WAY *of*

Reiki

WAY *of*
Reiki

Kajsa Krishni Boräng

Thorsons

Thorsons
An Imprint of HarperCollins*Publishers*
77–85 Fulham Palace Road
Hammersmith, London W6 8JB
The Thorsons website address is: www.thorsons.com

First published by Thorsons as *Principles of Reiki* 1997
This edition published by Thorsons 2001

1 3 5 7 9 10 8 6 4 2

© Kajsa Krishni Boräng 1997, 2001

Kajsa Krishni Boräng asserts the moral right
to be identified as the author of this work

A catalogue record for this book
is available from the British Library

ISBN 0 00 711019 7

Printed and bound in Great Britain by
Martins the Printers Limited, Berwick upon Tweed

Photograph on page 37 by Ametist Summanen

Contents

Acknowledgements

First of all I would like to thank my mother who is the base of my whole being. She has supported me through all my adventures. With her open mind, she has been a great listener to all my tales. When I started teaching Reiki she was my first student.

I would like to thank Baba Muktananda, my Spiritual Teacher, who opened my heart and connected me to my inner being. He allowed me to learn Reiki in his ashram which made it possible for me to express my spirituality in a practical way. I also want to offer my gratitude to The One who continues to reveal the Truth to me.

I want to thank my Reiki Master Wanja Twan who taught me Reiki and with whom I have shared my fascination with energy work in many situations and in many different countries. With her earth mother quality and warm laughter, it is a pleasure to spend time with her.

I also feel very grateful to my Qi Gong Masters, Zhixing and Zhendi Wang, who have expanded my understanding about the workings of subtle energies.

On a practical note, thank you to everyone who brought me into this computer age. Thank you Mattias for my first lesson, Kerstin for teaching me to save, Ulf for spending a whole dinner party playing around with my computer, Bo for spending the train journey between Gothenburg and Malmö creating and destroying files, Håkan from V-data who helped me out when I got stuck in a file, my brother Egil for giving me a very cute printer, Laurie for printing and for being my personal computer tutor.

I appreciate the Reiki lunches and cappuccinos I shared with my Reiki buddy Martha Sylvester discussing the progress of this book.

A great thank you goes also to all my Reiki students whose experiences have helped to create this book. It has been a privilege and an inspiration to watch you change with the help of Reiki.

Finally, I would like to thank my agent Susan Mears and my editor Diana Shaw. Without them the book would not exist at all!

Thank you, thank you, thank you!

Foreword

'Hands on, Reiki on – hands off, Reiki off!' my teacher, Mrs Hawayo Takata used to say about Reiki.

These incredibly simple directions for healing fitted perfectly in my life when I met her in the late 1970s. At that time I was very busy on a big farm in British Columbia, Canada. Besides having many animals and a family of eight to attend to, I had a weaving school and was involved in the local community by writing a small newspaper.

Having come from a big city, Stockholm, Sweden, to the country in Canada, over the years I had had to learn many practical household arts, including hunting and fishing, gardening, food preserving, animal husbandry, bee keeping, butter and cheese making, baking, sewing, knitting – everything you need to sustain life.

When Mrs Takata came to the area where I lived and presented a Reiki course, I found that it was another natural step to take.

Mrs Takata said: 'All you have to do is take your hands out, apply, and you heal. And as far as healing is concerned, you don't worry, because you are not doing it, the energy is doing it, Reiki is doing it. If Reiki is doing it there is no mistake, you understand?'

That felt very good, easy and practical to me!

'Treat yourself first – your family first and then your friends, you know. That is a good system, yeah. Because if your family is not well and you go outside and do Reiki, Reiki, and try to get people's "Thank you, thank you!", that is just expressing your ego, you know. You want to hear the word "thank you", you see. But your family can say "thank you"! If your family prove that they are well and strong and happy, what more do you want? That is the height of your beautiful home. Reiki has come into your home and therefore you are all happy. So this is the way I have tried to do it in my family, too. So – when I learned I came home and set all my family straight! Nobody died after that, only of old age!'

I listened to Mrs Takata's many wonderful stories of healing through her art of laying on of hands and her explanation of the Reiki healing energy.

She said: 'If you do not have Reiki, you are using the little bit of energy that you are born with, you don't have this energy that is space. This is – nobody can figure out how big this is. This is so big, so big, because it is God's power. You cannot see God, you see? But He still governs the Universe. How many years now? He has never stopped and that's the same thing. He is the one that can give you the energy in you. And – He is telling us to use it! If you use it, you get results! When you get results, just look up and say: "Thank you, God!" That's all you want to say. Yeah, and you get more bonus very soon.'

Mrs Takata taught Reiki as an oral tradition, with the energy to be passed on from hand to hand. The successful results of the Reiki treatments was the proof of its effectiveness.

In Canada Mrs Takata passed on her knowledge of the Reiki healing tradition to Barbara Brown, Ursula Baylow, Richard Bockner, Bethal Phaigh and Wanja Twan when she made them Reiki Masters in 1979–80. Mrs Takata's very last visit to Canada was in October of 1980.

This spring, in a Distant Healing class in Sweden, a lady asked me if we could possibly send some mental healing to her dog. She told me that over the years the dog had become stronger and stronger, and was forever pulling her along when they went on their daily walks. 'I used to enjoy going out with her, but now I am worried that I will fall over. Nothing has helped, she has gone to dog-obedience school, I have used the appropriate commands, I just don't know what to do anymore.'

The small, slender woman was obviously distraught, so we agreed that this was a good case to do some healing practice on. For about fifteen minutes we focused on the dog, and then went on to other matters. After that we enjoyed tea and some social time together. The dog owner decided she had to make a phone call home, and went out to do so. When she came back into the room she looked exalted when she called out to us: 'It worked, it worked!'

By that time we were engrossed in a discussion, so we all looked up at her surprised and said, 'What worked?'

'My dog, my dog!' she said. 'My daughter told me on the phone that a very strange thing had happened on her walk with the dog earlier today. She had been rushing along, pulling hard as usual, but then she suddenly stopped and looked quizzically at my daughter. She waited for her to catch up, and then walked at her side the rest of the way home! She has never done that before. I am so happy!'

'Yes,' I said, 'that is great. Like Takata said – Reiki works, Reiki does it. Thank you, God!'

Wanja Twan
November 1996
Kaslo, British Columbia, Canada

Introduction

Since Reiki is an oral tradition, it is very hard to write a book about it. You can not teach or learn Reiki through a book. The basis of Reiki, as in many other oriental traditions, is the direct transmission of energy from teacher to student – called initiation. This is what takes place in a Reiki workshop.

So what can I tell you here? I can recreate what traditionally happens in a Reiki workshop – the telling of stories. How it all started. How I came in contact with Reiki. My experience with Reiki.

So here is my story …

ONE

MY STORY

In the autumn of 1969 I found myself in India looking for a spiritual teacher or a yoga system.

I was a psychology student from Sweden who had grown more and more disappointed in my subject. My restlessness manifested itself as a lot of travelling. During one of my journeys in the Middle East I caught typhoid fever. While recovering I got quite depressed and started to question the importance of my studies. This in turn led me to question everything I did and life in general. Talking to a psychologist about all my existential questions, I realised he did not know more about life than I did. This was a real turning point for me; I decided to go to India and find answers there myself.

Whenever I heard of something interesting happening somewhere, I would go and investigate. I saw people walking on fire and I experienced the energy of a yogi who had been sitting on a tiger skin in the jungle for 12 years. I even saw a yogi known for producing ashes out of his hand. Yet none of this touched me inside.

After five months of searching, I heard about a powerful yogi who gave blessings to devotees and seekers on a roof terrace in Bombay. His name was Baba Muktananda. Just to sit in his presence filled me with elation, and I left with a big grin on my face and my feet hardly touching the ground.

I decided to go to the morning meditation that he gave in a smaller group. It was a small room, the energy was thick, as if you could cut the air with a knife. A few people around him were deep in meditation. Baba was sitting in a chair reading a book with sunglasses on, as if what was going on in the room had nothing to do with him. I was mystified.

Suddenly I could feel the energy closing in on myself. I started to cry and cry and cry – it was like an internal monsoon. The tears were not of sadness, but like a release of tension from my whole life and maybe lifetimes. Then I had this strong message inside me: 'This is what you have been looking for.' It felt like a home-coming. As far as rational thinking goes, I did not have a clue about what was happening. My only thought when I came out of the room was, 'Wow, where does this man live? What is his address?'

This powerful initiation from a realized Master was the awakening of my own inner energy. My spiritual journey had begun and I had many profound spiritual experiences. I kept coming back to India and spending more and more time in Baba Muktananda's ashram.

In the ashram, a beautiful place filled with animals and gardens, everybody had a different task to perform. Doing these practical jobs was a form of spiritual practice called seva, or selfless service. One day as I was helping in the deer park, Baba came by to feed the deer. He stopped and looked very intensely at me and said: 'Krishni, you look after the deer. Love the deer, lose yourself in the deer, think about nothing but the deer, and the deer will love you back and follow you around the whole ashram.' I took this seva as a form of meditation and more or less lived with the deer for six years.

The ashram children saw me as one of the deer. If they saw me outside the deer park, they would ask 'Who let you out?' I raised a young fawn on goat's milk, and when we walked around the ashram together, I would hear a child say 'There goes Shivaya and his mum.'

In the autumn of 1981 the deer fell ill. They had caught foot-and-mouth disease, a contagious viral infection. If this had taken place in the West, the whole herd would have been slaughtered. It was

3

Kajsa Krishni Boräng with the deer in the ashram

very painful for me to watch one animal after another get thinner and thinner and finally fall down, never to stand up again. When I approached Baba, he seemed curiously uninterested. I was thrown back on my own inner strength; afterwards I understood that he wanted me to learn something.

I started to pray for a solution, which in my mind would have been an Indian vet – not so easy to come by. Instead a big blonde woman, who had just arrived in the ashram, started talking to me. Her name was Wanja Twan, she was Swedish like myself and I felt an instant connection with her. She told me that she was a healer and offered to teach me her system called Reiki.

I knew I had to ask for permission from Baba to learn this healing system. Having heard his lectures about people trying to help others when they could not even help themselves, I was certainly very hesitant to ask. I had also seen a lot of 'burnt out' psychotherapists and healers coming to the ashram. Meanwhile, Wanja herself just went straight up to Baba and asked if she could teach me Reiki. To my surprise he immediately said yes.

Wanja started her teaching by giving me the four initiations necessary for the first degree Reiki. I could feel some energy going through me, but I cannot say that I believed it would work. It was only when I started practising Reiki that I realized that the changes that took place happened first inside *me*.

I had separated one little fawn from his sick mother, so he would not catch the disease. Unfortunately he already had. After I was initiated, I started treating him. Holding him in my lap and putting my hands on him, I immediately felt enveloped in a bubble of love. One night I felt he was dying but I was totally calm, totally centred and at peace with the situation and myself. This was completely different from how I felt when the other deer died. I kept giving the fawn Reiki. Suddenly he seemed to want to crawl into me, he let out a sound and I watched his spirit leave his body and brighten up the room. I could sense his gratitude pulsating in the room. It was a very beautiful experience.

The next day when I told Baba that one more deer had died, he said with such simplicity and so much love in his voice, 'They come and they go. What do you want me to do?' He was totally detached, he was such a free being. I was the one who had taken all this responsibility about life and death on myself. With the Reiki I could give without limit and I did not have to think about the result. It had nothing to do with me. This was quite a learning experience!

The rest of the deer herd recovered their health with the Reiki treatments. Wanja and I used to put our hands in their drinking water to energize the water with Reiki. One deer named Mamata, who was quite tame, had the disease as badly as the deer that had died. We put a bucket of carrots in front of her and treated her 'hands on' for an hour every day for about a month. It was incredible to watch her change. To start with Mamata was extremely thin, partly because she could not eat and partly because the other deer chased her away to protect themselves. Her fur was sticky and she had the bedraggled posture of a sick animal. As we gave her Reiki, she perked up little by little. She stopped drooling, which was one of the major symptoms. Her fur started to shine again. Most interesting of all, she regained her 'spark' and started to defend herself and bite back against the other deer. In fact, Mamata became queen of the herd!

For the deer that would not stand still for 'hands on' healing, I had to learn 'distant healing', which is part of second degree Reiki.

Wanja and I used to sit in the deer park sending energy to the deer that still had symptoms. As the energy went in we could actually see the animals shake a bit. When all the deer were healed from foot-and-mouth disease I continued to treat them for the many kinds of wounds they got from fighting during the mating season. It was amazing to see how serious wounds healed quite quickly with Reiki.

After a while I also started to treat humans. I was not at all prepared for the powerful experiences that people went through during their Reiki healing sessions. Each was personal according to what the person needed. When I put my hands on people, they often had a lot of emotional release, such as crying. Sometimes people remembered very early traumatic childhood memories, or even past lives. Some people just fell asleep, but woke up quite refreshed.

In the beginning I did not feel much myself while treating, which did not seem to matter at all. As I kept practising, I started to pick up more and more with my hands and later with my body. Sometimes, while treating somebody, phrases would enter my head or I would get intuitive knowledge about the person's problem. It was all very exciting!

Back in Sweden in the autumn of 1984, I spent time travelling with Wanja, who was giving Reiki workshops. One evening she initiated me as a Reiki Master, the third degree of Reiki that enabled me to teach Reiki, to give the initiation. It was a very emotional moment.

Since then I have studied, and continue to study, many other healing and educational systems that work with subtle energy such as the Alexander Technique, Qi Gong and Acupuncture. But for me, Reiki is the underlying factor.

So what is Reiki?

TWO

WHAT IS
Reiki?

There is only one energy

Reiki is a Japanese word in which the first syllable, Rei, means spirit, aura or subtle energy. The second syllable, Ki, means energy or power. Different cultures and spiritual paths have different names for this energy. In China it is called Qi and in India, Shakti or Prana. In English we use terms such as life-force, cosmic consciousness or divine energy.

The words Reiki and energy are interchanged deliberately throughout the book to show the universal existence of this energy apart from any specific tradition.

Hawayo Takata, one of the Reiki Grand Masters, wrote in her early diary:

> *I believe there exists One Supreme Being – the Absolute Infinite – a Dynamic Force that governs the world and universe. It is an unseen spiritual power that vibrates and all the other powers fade into insignificance beside it. So, therefore, it is Absolute!*
>
> *This power is unfathomable, immeasurable, and being a universal life force, it is incomprehensible to man. Yet, every single living being is receiving its blessings daily, awake or asleep.*
>
> *Different teachers and masters call Him the Great Spirit; the Universal Life Force; Life Energy, because when applied it vitalises the whole system; Ether Wave because it soothes pain and puts you into deep slumber as if under an*

anaesthetic; and the Cosmic Wave because it radiates vibrations of exultant feeling and lifts you into harmony.

I shall call it Reiki because I studied under that expression.

Channelling Reiki

Reiki as a method is a hands-on healing system for channelling this Life Force. The way of learning Reiki is through initiations, where the student is connected up as a channel by a Reiki Master. The person giving Reiki channels the energy through her body and out of her hands.

Because of the channelling there is no use of the practitioner's own energy. The Reiki energy is universal and has no limits. When the Reiki goes through the practitioner, he is actually receiving a treatment at the same time as he is giving one. The initiation and the connection to the Reiki lineage protect the practitioner from taking on any bad or sick energy from the patient. This connection also protects the patient from any negative energy from the practitioner. The only thing that is channelled is pure energy – Reiki. This is why it is such a safe system. To illustrate the last point, I would like to give an example.

Once I was in a bad mood when I was going to treat one of my friends. He told me that he did not want any angry vibrations in his body. I told him he was not getting my energy, he was getting pure Reiki. As soon as I put my hands on his head, I could feel the energy coming through, calming and settling my energy at the same time as he was receiving his treatment.

Reiki is an Intelligent Force

Reiki is an intelligent force. It goes where the body needs it, not just the area under the practitioner's hands. There is a foundation treatment in which hands are placed in different positions on the patient's body, but you can give a whole treatment with the hands in one position. Often I treat friends or family members while we are having a conversation by just putting my hands on their feet or shoulders. It is a kind of 'social' Reiki that brings another dimension into our relationship.

There is also no need to guide the Reiki with the mind, in fact this energy is much higher than the mind. Takata used to say 'hands on Reiki on, hands off Reiki off'. The fact that it is so simple seems to be the most difficult thing for people to understand. People often ask me if I am concentrating or thinking anything special while I am giving a treatment, but I am not. Usually I fall into a kind of very pleasant meditative space when I connect to the Reiki.

Reiki works on all levels – spiritual, mental, emotional and physical. It is a total natural and holistic system, where the energy goes to the level where the problem exists in the patient. That is why people have so many different reactions during and after a treatment; it cleanses on all levels. Chronic cases and physical problems usually take longer to treat, since they have taken longer to manifest themselves in the body. Emotional and acute problems are quicker to move.

From a practical point of view, there is no need to undress the patient. Reiki goes through clothes, blankets and even plaster casts. I once treated somebody with his foot in a cast and he could feel the heat from my hands and energy moving inside the foot.

Reiki Stands Above any Belief System

Reiki stands above any dogma or belief system even though the man who rediscovered it was inspired by Christ's healing miracles and found the healing formula in a Buddhist Sanskrit scripture. It is not even necessary to believe in Reiki for it to work.

My sister Kerstin is a professional sceptic when it comes to unseen realities. Once when she had a headache I offered to treat her with Reiki. Though she did not believe that Reiki could possibly change anything, she agreed to a treatment. After her first Reiki session Kerstin had a shoulder ache instead of a head ache. She was very puzzled. I could tell that her headache was caused by tension in her shoulders. The second Reiki treatment released the shoulders and the pain disappeared.

Even after I taught Kerstin Reiki, she could not really accept that putting her hands on somebody could help them. When one of her friends had a headache, she offered to give her some Reiki saying that it probably would not work. The headache disappeared quite quickly, and my sister is still in shock.

The Essence of the Energy is Love

For me the essence of Reiki is love. As soon as I put my hands on someone, my heart opens up and I feel connected to the patient on a level far beyond personality. A pleasant energy, warm and tingling, spreads in my body and goes from my hands into the patient's body. I can feel how tension melts away under my hands. I always feel better after I have given a treatment because of my connection to the Reiki energy. Even when I treat people whom I might find difficult on a personal level, I only feel compassion.

Love has no discrimination. Love has no judgement. Love is.

THREE

INITIATION AND
Lineage

Initiation

Initiation, or transmission of energy, is the traditional way of learning in many oriental systems. Instead of putting more intellectual concepts into the mind, as we do here in the West when learning, initiation works directly on the student's energy level by opening up the student's own energy and intuition. The Reiki initiations also open up the student as a Reiki channel and connect him to this special tradition and lineage of healing.

Hawayo Takata, the Grand Master of Reiki who brought the system from Japan to the West, explained in an interview that she saw herself as the engineer or technician. She gave her pupils the contact with the great universal life force that does the healing, in the same way as you plug a new television into the socket to get energy. In this computer age I sometimes say, when asked about the initiation, that I link people up to the net. Everybody seems happy with that!

Once initiated, the initiations stay with you always, even if you never practise or use the Reiki consciously. It is like an irreversible programming. The Reiki flows automatically after the initiation whenever you touch somebody.

Wanja tells the story of how she initiated her sons into Reiki. They were in their twenties, and used to go out dancing. The initiations totally changed their dancing experience. Instead of making light-hearted, superficial conversation, their dance partners opened up to the touch of Reiki and poured out all their troubles to the sons. Coming home to Wanja, they jokingly asked her to reverse the process. Impossible!

Reiki Means Change

The word initiation means beginning. It is the opening up to some-thing new. It is a profound change of a person's subtle energy level. Not everybody who takes the Reiki initiations will work with heal-ing. Many people learn Reiki as part of a personal growth process or for self-healing. Some people channel Reiki through music, others into food. Whatever you touch or create reflects your energy level and who you are.

For some it is their first contact with spiritual energy which can lead to dramatic changes in their lives. It can be the opening up to a spiritual path, and a spiritual understanding of life. Practising Reiki can be combined with following any form of spiritual path. I have initiated people practising Yoga, Buddhism, Sufism, Qi Gong and Anthroposophy. It is easy because they already have a good under-standing of the mysterious and wonderful work of subtle energy. Some people are content with just practising Reiki. That is also fine.

Reactions Caused by the Initiations

Whatever the reason people have learned Reiki, they are bound to go through a clear out of personal 'stuff'. The strongest reactions usually happen after the first day of the Reiki workshop. The reac-tions differ very much depending on what people carry with them. People with a lot of physical problems usually have some aches and pains. Repressed emotions come to the surface. A common reaction is to feel incredibly tired because of all the subtle internal changes taking place. Once I had a student who slept through the whole workshop! I just woke him up when it was time for the initiations. Then he went back to sleep again.

Another common reaction is to feel 'spaced out' or ungrounded for a while. Once two of my students were stopped by the police while driving home from the first day of the workshop. They had to blow into a balloon to show that they were not drunk. These are some extreme reactions. Other people feel slightly elated or just very peaceful. Some people may not feel much at the time, but subtle changes have taken place that are hard to describe.

On a physical level, most students feel heat and tingling in the hands after the initiations. For others that might take time to manifest. I have noticed that students with a lot of muscular tension do not feel as much in the beginning. It is important to understand that the healing works regardless of the sensation in the hands of the practitioner. I remember a treatment that I received from Wanja's daughter Krissy when I had a cold. She was young, maybe about eleven at the time, her hands were small and cool and she could not quite remember the positions. I thought to myself, 'This is just not going to work.' But, surprise, surprise! The next morning I was well.

The purification after the initiation happens by itself. After two to three months the energy has settled.

A Delayed Reaction

A young man, Jocko, felt very angry with me after a Reiki workshop. He did not feel a thing and felt cheated. His friends and I tried to calm him down saying that he should wait and see. Some time later when I met him again he apologized and told me the following story.

About a month after the initiation, Jocko was woken up in the middle of the night by some light phenomena in his room.

The next day when walking to school he went into another reality. Jocko felt incredibly connected to nature. His hearing was most affected of all his senses: Jocko heard every detail in nature – the ants crawling, the grass growing. He thought to himself, 'What is this, so strange and so beautiful?' He felt as though he was transcending time and space.

Even as his experience faded away he was left with a clearer vision.

Experiences During the Initiations

What happens during the initiations is also very individual. Experiences vary from having visions to seeing colours, feeling energy going through the body, being very moved emotionally or feeling not much at all. One woman felt sad during an initiation. She told me she heard the phrase inside her: 'You always wanted to do this. Why did you wait so long?'

We usually do not discuss what happens too much during the workshop, since the students may start comparing notes instead of feeling happy with their own unique experiences.

Reiki works regardless of the kind of reaction that the student has during and after the initiation. Reiki is a very democratic system: everybody can learn it! Since Reiki has nothing to do with the mind, even children as young as four years old can have the initiations.

Usually these are children of parents who practise Reiki, who want to learn what their parents do.

Special Gifts Coming from the Initiations

Occasionally special psychic abilities develop spontaneously after the Reiki initiations. The most recent example of this that I have come across is Anne-Marie in Lyon. Shortly after her initiations for the first degree, she started to wake up around three o'clock in the morning, feeling prompted from inside to get up and write. First she resisted, but then she got up and started to write in an automatic manner. What she received was information regarding problems with her friends, family or patients that she was treating so that she could help them better.

To give some examples – Anne-Marie had been worried about her daughter's progress in school because she did not seem to be doing well. The writings told her that her daughter was dyslexic and that she should contact the school to get her daughter the right support. Without giving the source of the information, Anne-Marie went to the school and told them about her suspicion of her daughter's dyslexia. When tested, her daughter was indeed found to be dyslexic and was given adequate support.

Another time, when Anne-Marie's daughter was on a school trip, Anne-Marie started to feel uneasy. During the night in her inspired writing, she was told that her daughter's classmates were not being very nice to her. Anne-Marie was told to write to her daughter and tell her not to pay any attention or respond to the teasing. Both of them were also to pray for protection. When she received the letter, the daughter was utterly amazed about how her mother could know exactly what was happening.

When I met Anne-Marie recently while she was learning the second degree Reiki, I asked her half jokingly if she had any messages for me during the night. She said no, but when I was back in London she phoned me to say that she had received information for me on the following night. Some days later I received two printed pages giving me the message.

The message said that I could incorporate the following passage in this book, and I quote:

> ... *that these kinds of phenomena or contact can*
> *take place. But it would be more correct, even if it*
> *is just a matter of labelling, to talk about inspired*
> *writing rather than automatic writing. In fact,*
> *inspired writing comes from celestial entities,*
> *who in their dimension are the artists and helpers*
> *in the divine work, whom one can also call*
> *'beings of light', whereas automatic writing can*
> *have other sources.*

It was signed, 'The Angels'.

Lineage

Often, when we learn an oriental system, we talk about lineage. This is the base of many healing traditions including Qi Gong, Tai Chi, Yoga, Reiki and other similar spiritual practices. These systems are several thousand years old, not recent discoveries. As 'living knowledge' that has been passed down and practised from teacher to teacher, the purpose of the traditions may vary from self-realization to spiritual healing systems. We always respect the teachers as carriers of the energy of the tradition.

The lineage of teachers supports us in our healing work and in our lives.

These concepts might be difficult for a Westerner to understand, so I will illustrate them by telling a story.

A Room in a Cloud

I was treating Ellen, a friend of mine, with Reiki for a digestive problem. One night she dreamt that I took her flying up to a room in a cloud. I left her there with a 'bossy' Japanese woman and flew away. My friend was quite annoyed with me. The woman, who was casually dressed in a T-shirt, pointed to some large cushions on the floor for Ellen to sit down. She spoke in a staccato kind of voice, quite terse and to the point. Turning to Ellen she said sharply, 'Why are you not well? We have been working on your case for such a long time!'

She pulled out a book describing Ellen's whole case history. She then proceeded to treat Ellen by waving her hands up and down several times in front of Ellen's body. A tremendous amount of energy and light was released into Ellen's body, and this continued in her sleep. When she woke up the next morning she felt energized and had the feeling that something really significant had taken place. This experience gave Ellen the insight that she had to take better care of herself.

I felt the description of the Japanese woman matched Wanja's description of Hawayo Takata so I showed Ellen a picture of Takata that she had never seen before – it was the same woman!

Another function of the lineage is to keep the teachings pure. It is the same unchanged knowledge coming down from teacher to teacher. To show this understanding of Reiki as a spiritual practice with a lineage and not just a healing method, we sometimes call it 'The Usui System of Reiki Healing' instead of just Reiki. This is also to honour Dr Mikao Usui as the Grand Master and founder of this healing system.

The importance of the lineage is also the reason why we keep repeating the stories of the Grand Master's lives in every Reiki workshop. Even these stories carry an energy and a message.

So, let me tell you the history of Reiki as I have heard it from my teacher Wanja Twan, as she heard it from her teacher Hawayo Takata, who listened to her teacher Chujiro Hayashi, who in his turn was the student of Mikao Usui.

Are you ready?

FOUR

HISTORY OF REIKI
– the Lineage

Reiki is a method of healing that dates back about 2500 years, but was forgotten for a very long time. In the nineteenth century the system was rediscovered by a man called Dr Mikao Usui. This is the story of his discovery.

Dr Mikao Usui's Story

Dr Mikao Usui was the headmaster of a Christian boys' school in Kyoto, Japan, towards the end of the nineteenth century. He also used to deliver the sermons on Sundays. One Sunday morning, some of his students approached him and asked him if he really believed in what he was teaching. They wanted to know if he believed that the Bible stories of Jesus' miracles, and especially his healing, were literally true. Usui answered that yes, he did believe that Jesus performed miracles and healed people. The students then wanted Usui to demonstrate how Jesus did his healing. They said that they were too young to believe, they needed proof!

Usui took their demands seriously. He said, 'I do not know how to do healing now, but I will find out. When I know how to do it, I will return and tell you.' The next day, Usui left his post at the university in search of the answers to these questions.

Feeling that the missionaries who trained him had not taught him everything, Dr Usui wanted to explore his religion in a Christian country and went to the United States to study theology at a University of Chicago. Dr Usui studied the Bible and the Christian scriptures, but nowhere could he find what he was looking for – a formula for how Jesus did his healing. Knowing that Buddha also healed the sick, he started to study Buddhism. After seven years in America, Dr Usui decided to return to Kyoto in Japan, an area

Dr Mikao Usui

known for its many Buddhist temples. There, he would have more Buddhist scriptures available for study.

Back in Kyoto, Dr Usui visited many monasteries. Yet many Buddhist monks did not seem interested in his questions on healing. They said that they were more interested in the purification of the mind than of the body. Finally Dr Usui found a Zen Abbot who said that he was interested in Dr Usui's search and invited him to stay and study in his monastery outside Kyoto.

Dr Usui started to study the Buddhist Scriptures, the sutras, in Japanese. Since Buddhism came to Japan through China, he learned Chinese to have more scriptures available to him. Later Dr Usui learned Sanskrit, the sacred and ancient language of India, where Buddha was born. Only then did he come across a formula, some symbols that described how Buddha did his healing. Dr Usui had finally found what he was looking for, but he felt that as he did not know how to use the symbols, he did not have the power to heal.

To achieve a healing power from inside, Usui decided to meditate and fast on the sacred mountain, Kurayama, seventeen miles outside Kyoto.

Dr Usui's Experience on the Mountain

Having climbed the mountain, Dr Usui settled down to meditate, chant and fast for twenty-one days. This, he hoped, would accomplish his task. To keep time, he put twenty-one stones in front of him. As each day passed, he threw away one stone.

Before dawn on the last morning, Usui saw a flickering light on the horizon. As it came closer, Dr Usui became quite frightened, but he decided to be courageous, to face it. This was his moment. This was what he had been waiting for. The light turned into a bright white beam that hit him between the eyes. It was so powerful that Dr Usui fell down, unconscious.

When Dr Usui regained consciousness, he looked up at the sky and saw bubbles of all the colours of the rainbow dancing in front of his eyes. Then the sky turned into a bright white screen. On that screen, Usui saw the symbols that he had found in the Sanskrit scriptures written in golden letters. As they vibrated in front of him, their use and meaning were transmitted to him and they seemed to say 'Remember, remember, remember!'

The Four Miracles of Reiki

When Usui came out of his experience, he was filled with light and energy, even though he had fasted for three weeks. That was the first sign for Dr Usui that he had received something on the mountain.

In his enthusiasm, Dr Usui rushed down the mountainside, stumbled and stubbed his toe which started bleeding. Automatically, he put his hand over the toe. The bleeding stopped and the pain went away. For Dr Usui, this was the second miracle of the healing energy of Reiki.

Coming down the mountain, Dr Usui saw an outdoor snack bar. As he had started to get hungry, he ordered a traditional Japanese breakfast. The old man serving the food saw from the length of Usui's beard that he had been fasting for quite some time. He wanted to serve Dr Usui some rice water to break the fast gently, but Usui insisted on a full meal. When the old man's granddaughter brought Usui his breakfast, he could see that her face was swollen and she had been crying. She told him that she was suffering from toothache from an infected tooth. Dr Usui put his hand on the aching tooth and the ache disappeared almost immediately. This was the third proof of the workings of the Reiki energy. The fourth miracle for Dr Usui was the fact that he could digest his whole breakfast without getting indigestion!

27

Dr Usui in the Slum Area

Returning to the monastery, Usui found the Abbot in bed with arthritis, hugging his blanket to his chest. As Dr Usui told him about his experiences, he put his hand on the abbot to relieve his pain. The next morning they discussed what Dr Usui should do with his new gift. After deciding that Dr Usui should give it to the people who needed it the most, he went to a large slum in Kyoto.

Dr Usui began by treating very poor people who supported themselves by begging. Once they were healed, Dr Usui wanted them to go to the Abbot in his old monastery to ask for a job and a new name so that they would find a new sense of identity and change their ways.

After many years of work in this slum area, Dr Usui started to recognize faces of some people whom he had treated a long time ago. When he asked them why they were back, they told him that it was much easier to keep begging than to work.

The Spiritual Precepts of Reiki

Dr Usui felt that he had totally failed. He should have listened to the monks who told him that you could not treat just the physical body. First he said, 'No more Reiki for free!' There was no appreciation and gratitude from the beggars. They were not ready to change and take responsibility for their lives.

Secondly, Usui added his spiritual precepts to the Reiki tradition:

Just for today do not anger.
Just for today do not worry.
Honour your parents, teachers and elders.
Earn your living honestly.
Show gratitude to all living things.

After this experience, Usui left the slums of Kyoto and went on a pilgrimage all over Japan. He used to carry a torch in broad daylight to make people curious. If people asked him why, he said that he was looking for people who needed light. Then he would give lectures about Reiki in the temples.

In this manner Usui met his successor, Churjiro Hayashi.

Dr Churjiro Hayashi

When Hayashi met Usui, he was a 45-year-old retired naval officer. Usui felt that Hayashi was much too young to be retired and encouraged him to follow him on his pilgrimage of healing and teaching around Japan. In this way, Hayashi became Usui's disciple and, after Usui's death, his successor and what we in the West would call the Grand Master.

Hayashi created a Reiki clinic in Tokyo where Hawayo Takata was later treated. It was a small clinic with only eight beds. The Reiki practitioners were all men who wore traditional kimonos while treating their patients. The clinic was open in the morning, and in the afternoon practitioners made home visits to people who were too ill to come to the clinic. Patients were also treated with herbs.

At the beginning of the Second World War, Hayashi could sense the

Dr Churjiro Hayashi

coming conflict between Japan and the United States. He did not want to be recalled to military service and be responsible for taking lives, since he had given his life to healing and saving lives. Hayashi invited his family and Reiki Masters to a tea ceremony in which he voluntarily died by withdrawing his life force after having declared Hawayo Takata as his successor.

Hawayo Takata's Story

Hawayo Takata, a Japanese woman, was born in 1900 on one of the Hawaiian islands. Her parents named her after the islands because they wanted her to become something great. When she was in her thirties her husband died, leaving her to bring up their two small daughters. Overwork and worry brought her many physical problems, including gallstones, asthma and a tumour. On the verge of a nervous breakdown, Takata prayed for guidance and had an experience of an inner voice telling her to first of all take care of her health.

Following this advice, Takata went to Japan to have surgery. She went to a hospital in Tokyo where the doctor in charge was a friend of hers, who had previously treated her spouse. Dr Maeda put her on a special diet for three weeks so she would gain some weight before the operation.

On the day of the surgery, when Takata was already on the operating table, she heard a voice inside her saying, 'The operation is not necessary.' Takata jumped off the operating table, creating quite a stir. When her doctor came, she asked him if there was an alternative to the operation. Dr Maeda's response was to ask her how much time she had, because an alternative treatment could take a long time, from months to a year. To show her eagerness, Takata doubled the time and said she could stay for two years. Then Dr Maeda took her to talk to his sister, the dietician at the hospital, who had been treated with Reiki while suffering from dysentery.

Takata's First Encounter with Reiki

The next day Takata was brought to Hayashi's nearby Reiki clinic. She was treated by two men dressed in traditional kimonos. The first thing she noticed was the heat from their hands. Takata thought they were connected to some electrical wires and started looking under the table, in the ceiling, and in the wide sleeves of one of the men's kimonos. He thought she needed a tissue but when she explained that she was looking for some kind of electrical device, he started laughing.

Hayashi came in to see what was happening. He then explained to Takata that the energy she felt was not electrical energy. It was Reiki, which is the Japanese word for Universal Life Energy. He said, 'This energy comes through me to you. These,' he held up his hands, 'are the electrodes. That force begins to revitalise and restore the balance of your entire system.'

Takata received treatments every day and was well in four months. She was so impressed with this healing system that she wanted to learn it, but was not allowed to because she was regarded as a foreigner. Reiki was a guarded Japanese tradition.

She pleaded her case – what would she do if she fell ill again in Hawaii? Hayashi gave in. He told Takata that, if she was willing to stay a year and work with him in the clinic, he would give her the initiations into the first degree of Reiki. Takata agreed and moved in to live with the Hayashi family.

Takata Brings Reiki to the West

After a year of work in the clinic, Takata received her second degree Reiki initiations and returned to the United States. Back in Hawaii, she started treating family and friends. In 1937 Hayashi and his daughter came for a six month visit to help Takata establish Reiki in Hawaii. In February 1938, Hayashi initiated Takata as a Reiki Master and returned to Japan.

Takata taught Reiki throughout the United States and Canada for over forty years. Only in 1975 did she start to initiate Reiki Masters. Before she died in December 1980, she had initiated 22 Reiki Masters. The process that she helped set in motion has created an explosion of Reiki around the world.

Takata used to say, 'With Reiki comes Health, Happiness, Prosperity and a Long Life.'

FIVE

WANJA TWAN, MY
Reiki Master

Wanja Twan was one of the 22 Reiki Masters initiated by Hawayo Takata before she died. I feel very privileged to have her as my teacher. This is the story of how she came to learn Reiki.

Wanja Twan was born in Sweden; she moved to Canada in her early twenties to marry. She had two children but divorced her husband after twelve years because he spent less and less time with her and the family.

Wanja married again and had two more children. Her second husband also brought two children with him from a previous marriage, so together they had six children. They kept a farm with cows and sheep by a river in British Columbia and Wanja held weaving classes in the barn. People would come for two weeks from all over to learn how to weave. They would learn other things too, like camping, cooking, and making butter. It was a very rich experience. A full life.

One spring morning her husband announced that he was leaving Wanja for another woman. At first it was quite a shock. But one day when she felt sorry for herself Wanja opened a book at random to find inspiration. The book fell open at the phrase: 'God did not make us to be sorrowful.' She used this statement as a base for contemplation. Wanja seemed so happy in the end that people suspected that she had wanted to get rid of her husband!

Feeling that a chapter in her life had finished, Wanja wanted to open herself to something new, something spiritual – maybe a yoga course, she thought. There was nothing like that going on at the time in her area. Somebody told Wanja about a healing course, and gave her a telephone number. Wanja was not too enthusiastic. Healing? She was not ill.

Finally Wanja made up her mind. She phoned and asked what kind of healing it was. Did she need to know anything in order to take the course? How much did it cost? A friendly lady answered all her questions. The healing was called Reiki and the method was the laying on of hands. No, she did not need to know anything in advance. Anybody could learn it. Mrs Takata, the teacher, said that she is like a television technician putting the antennae on people. The course consisted of four sessions that last for about two hours each. The cost was 125 dollars. As Wanja listened to the last sentence, she heard a woman's voice in the background saying, 'That is American dollars, not Canadian!' Wanja thought to herself that it was quite a bit of money. It was about the same amount that one of her weaving students would pay for a two week course.

When Wanja asked around, nobody had heard about a healing method called Reiki. She then went to her bookcase full of second-hand spiritual books, pulled out a book and opened it at random. To her amazement, she started to read an interview with Takata. The book was *We Are All Healers*, written by Sally Hammond. She described how she had met Takata, a lively Japanese lady dressed in bright red, at a healing convention. Takata told her about her Reiki, her healing method. The writer ends the interview with the regret that she did not take Takata's address so she could have learned the system herself! This experience convinced Wanja to take the course.

Now only the money was missing. Miraculously, Wanja found exactly the right amount of money in a small desk drawer – she had been putting it there while saving to buy hay for the animals.

The night before the Reiki course Wanja was lying in bed gazing at a star. Suddenly it started moving with great speed, entering into her forehead like a brilliant explosion.

Phyllis Lei Furumoto, Hawayo Takata and Wanja Twan in Canada

The next day as Wanja entered the house where the course was held, Takata greeted her with the words, 'I knew you would come!' Wanja felt a bit shaken up by all this. How could she know?

After Wanja learned Reiki she started treating her animals, family and friends with good results.

In 1978, Wanja took her whole family on a Christmas vacation to Hawaii. Still interested in some kind of meditation, she brought the address, given to her by a friend, of a meditation group. The head of this meditation group happened to be visiting. His name was Baba Muktananda.

This meeting lead Wanja to have many powerful spiritual experiences that you can read about in her autobiography, *In the Light of a Distant Star*. It also led to me meeting Wanja in Baba Muktananda's ashram in India about three years later.

In the summer of the following year Takata returned to British Columbia to teach distance healing, the second degree of Reiki. Wanja took this class. She felt that if you started something you should follow it through to the end. Wanja also brought her daughters and oldest son to learn first degree Reiki. This time, Wanja had the opportunity to spend more time with Takata. She used to give Takata treatments and Takata encouraged and told Wanja to continue with the Reiki and become a Reiki Master.

One day in Wanja's weaving class, one of her students did not feel well. Wanja took her up to her house to give her a treatment. The woman showed Wanja all the medication that she was taking, saying that still she could not sleep at night. Wanja was shocked to see all the different pills and tablets, being in good health herself. She proceeded to give the woman treatments three days in a row. Even after the first treatment, she had a good night's sleep. As the woman was leaving, Wanja promised to send her some distant healing. Wanja later received a letter from the woman saying that she felt wonderful, she had no more pain!

This experience convinced Wanja that it was much more important to teach people about their health than to teach them weaving! She decided to take up Takata's offer to make her a Reiki Master.

In mid-October Takata came back to initiate a few Masters, one of them being Wanja. Wanja had organized big classes of both first and second degree Reiki for Takata to teach. Because there were so many children who wanted to learn, there was a special class for them.

When Takata initiated Wanja to Reiki Master, she told her that she had known all along that this was going to happen. She instructed Wanja in how to do the classes and how to give the initiations. Takata stressed the importance of starting to work with your own family, and the people in need close to you. Another point of importance was the exchange for a treatment – it did not need to be money. It could be a loaf of bread, just something to show some appreciation and that the person valued your time. Takata also discussed with Wanja that being a Master meant that you had to master the physical plane as well, which Wanja had done by organizing such big classes with so much ease.

Later that autumn Wanja and her family left the farm to move into a house in the Kootenays mountain range in British Columbia. Before moving there she had seen a blue house in a vision. Somehow she managed to find it and miraculously it was available! In this house Wanja started her healing work. She became quite well known in the area for giving treatments and Reiki classes.

Wanja in the Ashram

Wanja came to India in 1981 to spend three months in the company of Baba Muktananda who was in residence in his ashram at the time. Because she had her two daughters with her, she was staying in the Upper Garden which was a short distance from the main buildings

39

and activities. As it happened, they stayed in a bungalow that was situated right behind the deer park.

Every time she went down to the temple to chant or meditate she passed me and the deer. We started talking. Apart from both being Swedish, our love for animals bonded us. After she taught me Reiki, she worked with me in the deer park for three months, healing the deer from foot-and-mouth disease. Wanja also wanted to teach me everything else she knew.

We were doing past life regressions, seeing our connection through many lifetimes, as teacher-student or grandmother-grandson, always doing healing together. It felt like a very deep and loving relationship beyond time.

Wanja taught me a lot about energy: how you can mentally tune into the energy of saints through their statues and pictures and receive information and have conversations with them. Being with Wanja felt a little like entering the world of Alice in Wonderland. She would see all these different beings – gods, nature spirits, energy lines – and describe them to me.

One thing Wanja wanted to teach me that I never took her up on was eating clouds to create a sunny day. While living in India I felt quite happy with a cloud now and then!

I stayed in the ashram with the deer. Wanja left but she always managed to be there for me if I had trouble with the deer. Her timing was always perfect.

Wanja in Sweden

When I returned to Sweden from the ashram in 1986, Wanja had already moved back there part time. Her mother and sister were living in Stockholm. Wanja initiated them into Reiki following Takata's advice to start the healing process with the people closest to you. She also bought a house in the country to use as a healing centre.

Wanja taught extensively in Sweden and in Finland where *Wanja's World*, a documentary about her life, was made by Finnish television. Before she returned to the Kootenays in Canada she had initiated some 20 Reiki Masters.

Wanja Back in Canada

At the moment Wanja is happily living in the Kootenays surrounded by her children, grandchildren and their cats and dogs, all of whom live nearby. As a matter of fact, Wanja had to escape to Vancouver while writing her book about her life to avoid people's demands on her and being a full time baby-sitter. Once, when I visited her we were, within minutes, lumbered with a litter of motherless kittens, one puppy (not house trained) and a hungry baby!

Wanja still travels widely teaching Reiki. She has been to Australia several times. Wanja also travels back and forth to Sweden, sometimes stopping in the UK. One of her more remarkable journeys was to Poland where she visited a nun whom she had initiated as a Reiki Master. This nun has a certificate on the wall from the Pope allowing her to practise Reiki!

SIX

A REIKI
Treatment

A Reiki treatment is normally given as hands-on healing, but it can also be given as distant healing. In this chapter I will describe a hands-on session.

The Foundation Treatment

The patient lies down on her back on a massage table or a futon on the floor. I prefer working on the floor since I feel more at ease moving around the patient's body on the floor. I sit in a good position with the spine straight, without being rigid, so the energy can flow with ease. The patient keeps her clothes on since the energy penetrates the clothes. Usually I keep a blanket nearby in case the patient feels cold. Often when a lot of emotions come up they are preceded by a feeling of cold, I have noticed. Being covered by a blanket can also help people feel safe.

I start the treatment on the head, putting my hands over the eyes and forehead. The Reiki immediately connects without any ceremonies or intentions on my part, and I can feel the tingling in my hands as they start to get warmer. I do not apply any pressure or hold them away from the body of the patient. In fact I am doing nothing at all! I just let the energy coming through me do the work. I can, myself, feel the pleasant flow of Reiki going through me into the patient as I am settling into the session. When the heat of my hands subsides I move to the next hand position. There can be other manifestations in my hands, but I move when I sense a stillness. Wanja used to say very casually, 'move when you get bored'! Very quickly the hands seem to find their own rhythm.

I continue the treatment down the front of the body and then ask the patient to turn over so I can treat the back, from the shoulders down to the sacrum. I end the treatment with an energy stroke down the spine to bring the patient's attention back to her body. At the end of the session a person is usually extremely relaxed; some people are almost asleep. I give the patient some time to come to, so as not to jolt her new, balanced state.

If a person has a lot of emotional release during a treatment, I tend to keep my hands on the head or heart position all through the treatment. It feels more as though I am there with her, in case she wants to talk about what she is experiencing. I try to avoid giving advice or calming people down. I let the energy do the work and remain as a supportive witness.

It is a personal choice if the client wants to talk or not. It does not affect the healing process, which happens on a much deeper level. Some people seem to have a need to verbalize what they are going through, like sorting themselves from chaos into order.

I once had a patient who was a good example of this:

The Young Man who Talked Himself into Balance

I met Ben at a meditation retreat where I was giving Reiki treatments. Ben appeared to be highly eccentric. He would either talk non-stop or walk around in a spaced out state, seemingly oblivious to what was going on around him. Whatever he did was too much or it was nothing at all. I gave him three to four Reiki sessions a week for about a month.

As I started my first session with Ben, he started to talk and talk and talk. He described his childhood with a raving, mad mother who was trying to pull her son into destructive manipulative plots against his weak father. Ben's only defence was to stay completely aware of what was happening. He was extremely articulate. Ben talked himself through weeks of Reiki sessions. Sometimes he would look up at me and ask, 'What do you think?'

I had to answer honestly, 'I do not think, I am just listening.'

My Spiritual Teacher once said that people who talk a lot do so because they have never been really listened to. I decided to test this on Ben. During and after a particular session I kept listening uninterruptedly without really feeding the conversation, just an occasional hm or yeah.

After five hours Ben's voice started to slow down. Finally he said, 'I don't think that I have anything more to say.'

About a month later people approached me asking me what I had done to Ben, he seemed so normal. I had to admit the truth, 'Nothing!' He did it all himself with the help of Reiki.

Length and Frequency of Treatments

A Reiki treatment usually lasts between an hour and one-and-a-half hours. The energy keeps moving in the body after the treatment for about 24 hours. Because of this, it is common practice to give three to four treatments on consecutive days.

It is starting a process. Every Reiki session is different, with each session you reach deeper into the person. To have decided on at least three sessions to start with also works as a safety net for people who have very strong reactions during or after the first session, if the energy has stirred up a lot of 'stuff'. The second session will smooth this over and the practitioner can explain about the benefits of a clear-out. During the third treatment people usually feel quite good.

Depending on the particular problem you can then decide to have a treatment once or twice a week. There is no set pattern, except the more serious the problem, the more Reiki is needed.

Wanja told me about somebody who was badly burned all over his body. He received Reiki around the clock from all his Reiki friends with excellent results. There is never any risk from getting too much Reiki!

Acute or First Aid Treatment

There are situations where it is not convenient to lie a person down, or there is not time for an hour-long treatment. Reiki does not depend on the position of the body. It is only that lying down is more comfortable for the patient, if it is possible. When somebody has hurt himself, by shutting a hand in a door for example, Reiki is excellent first aid. You take the injured part between the hands, and hold them there until the pain subsides. It is also good to place the hands on the heart area for a while to treat the shock that an injury causes to the system. The injured area is normally much less bruised and swollen after Reiki.

A dramatic incident happened recently that can illustrate how great it can be to have 'magical hands'.

Aage, the husband of a woman who organised a Reiki course for me, had a heart condition. It felt natural to offer Aage two initiations before we went to the course and two when we got back, so he could treat himself.

When Aage came to pick us up from the house in the country where we held the workshop, he was very excited, and told us the following story. The same Sunday he went to church. Suddenly the man on the bench in front of him keeled over and hit his head on the back of the pew. My half-initiated student pulled the man towards him and started treating his heart. When the man came to, Aage took him outside for some fresh air, and later the priest came out to give the man communion. Aage thought it was curious that, out of the 400 people in the church, he was the one sitting right behind the man.

Easing the pain of headaches with an 'on the spot treatment' can also be very convenient. Holding the hands on a person's head and shoulders for about fifteen minutes is usually enough for the headache to subside. It can be very impressive.

Experiences During a Treatment

What people experience during a treatment varies a lot according to what each person needs at that moment and how sensitive he or she is to subtle energy. Some people may just feel a general relaxed state of being. They may need more treatments for the energy to penetrate deeper. Others with more acute problems can have quite strong reactions during the first session.

When I first started giving Reiki treatments, I was surprised by the number of people who started crying when I had my hands on their heart area. Sometimes they would know why they were crying, but often it is just an energy release.

On a physical level there will be heat, tingling or aching in problem areas, but after a while any tension will be smoothed out. When the muscles relax they might twitch, as they do sometimes before you go to sleep. The breathing pattern changes and the breath comes from a much deeper level. The Reiki treatment puts people into a kind of meditative state that gives them a profound relaxation – some people feel so relaxed that they go to sleep, which is quite OK. This sleep is much more beneficial than normal sleep.

As the Reiki connects people more to themselves, unresolved issues and memories from early life, or even past lives, might surface in order to be resolved. You can, as a practitioner, watch patients regress spontaneously and relive these events with the Reiki as support. I will give a few quite dramatic examples of this.

An Asthma Attack

I have treated patients with acute asthma and breathing problems. Usually the body relaxes, the anxiety level goes down and they breathe better.

One particular woman whom I was treating with Reiki was on heavy medication to suppress any asthma attacks. In the middle of the session she had the most terrible attack of asthma. I calmly kept doing the Reiki, in the full knowledge that whatever the Reiki would bring up the Reiki would calm down again. It could only be beneficial. The session lasted for about two hours until she could breathe properly.

She told me afterwards that she relived the experience of her mother dying in the same room as she was in when she was a teenager. When her mother took her last breath gasping for air, she must unconsciously have thought, 'This could happen to me too!' At that moment she had her first asthma attack. She had never seen or remembered that connection before.

A Birth Experience

When I was treating a friend called Amanda with a series of Reiki sessions, she seemed to regress with each treatment, to become younger and younger. Amanda saw images of herself lying in a pram. Even her appearance had a sort of baby-like quality. She would look around with big eyes while playing with her saliva with her tongue.

Suddenly during one session Amanda became completely limp. I asked her, 'What is happening?' She said she felt that she was back in her mother's womb and she could hear a man's voice saying, 'Keep pushing Mrs Jones, keep pushing!'

Amanda went back to her mother to ask about her birth. Indeed, it had been a difficult birth, in which the contractions stopped at a crucial moment towards the end, and her mother had to be given drugs to induce the continuation of labour.

Moving Back in Time

I treated Leonard, a man sitting in a wheelchair, once a week for a long time. I was not trying to cure him, I just treated him to keep up his energy levels. Leonard also had quite a weak spleen with pain and bloating.

One time, as I had my hands on his spleen, he had a vivid visual experience, accompanied by smells and very strong emotions.

Leonard experienced his left side, where the spleen is situated, being pierced by a spear. As the healing session proceeded, a landscape opened up and Leonard saw himself bleeding to death on a battlefield outside Rome. He was the head of the personal guards for a Roman general. Lying there, Leonard felt the shame of defeat, of not being able to have defended his commander and his honour. He had been the last man standing. His death meant the General would die too.

Leonard was also deeply worried about his wife who would be left by herself to take care of their three children on their farm. He also felt deeply saddened not to be able to see his children growing up.

Even after the healing session ended, he kept seeing flashes of this previous life all through the day and night. Leonard also saw his body, surrounded by his weapons, being burned on a fire.

After that experience, over a period of several years the pain and discomfort he had felt in that area disappeared completely.

These kinds of negative memories are stored in the body on a subtle level. It takes a lot of energy to hold these memories. When we can let go, there is a surge of energy in the body.

Reiki as Meditation

People can have Reiki treatment without having any particular problem. Their experiences might be more like meditation experiences
because Reiki is a spiritual force. I actually had somebody come to
me for treatments because he did not feel in contact with his inner
being.

On that level, the experience might be an altered state of consciousness, seeing bright colours or light, feeling an openness of
heart, having visions and even hearing mantras.

Of course experiences happen at many levels at the same time,
since we are an organic, whole system.

Reactions After a Reiki Treatment

The reactions to a Reiki treatment can also vary greatly depending
on the kind of problem a person has. If somebody has a particu-
larly strong reaction – feeling sick, feeling aches and pains, having
a blazing headache, etc. – I usually ask, 'Have you had this problem before?' This always turns out to be the case.

Reiki is very good at detecting weaknesses of the body, in order to
strengthen them. Reiki does not put anything in, Reiki cleans things
out! The difference between a reaction and a normal disease is that
a reaction lasts for a very short time and occurs within 24 hours of
the treatment.

Reiki works like a flood of energy, moving blocks, increasing the circulation on both a subtle and physical level, and balancing the system.

On a physical level, toxic waste accumulated in the body is cleared out. Common physical reactions after a treatment are: having to go to the loo more often, the urine being darker than normal, sweat with a bad odour, more mucus, feeling aches in places where there have previously been problems, such as surgery or broken bones. Some people feel flu-like symptoms.

On an emotional level, people might feel vulnerable or irritable or some feelings of old sadness might surface. It is extremely common to feel tired, or sometimes to become aware of and acknowledge your actual state of being.

All these more negative reactions are more common after the first treatment or in the beginning of a series of treatments. If we understand that they are a healing crisis that is part of a purification process, it is easier to have a positive outlook.

On a more positive note, people feel calmer, more relaxed, and have a sense of spiritual wellbeing after a Reiki treatment.

Problems that Respond Well to Reiki

All emotional problems respond very quickly to Reiki. Physical problems that are directly linked to stress and tension also respond well because of the centring and balancing effect of Reiki at a very deep level. As a matter of fact, most of my early clients had emotional problems or bad backs. A back that had 'gone out' or into spasm would usually be relieved within three treatments. Headaches, cramps, sleeping problems and high blood pressure also belong to this category. Anything like emotions, stress or tension that move into the body can quite quickly also leave it. After all, everything is just energy.

The mother of one of my students was in hospital waiting for surgery because her intestines were cramped into a knot. Her daughter had just learned Reiki and went to visit. She discreetly put her hands on her mother's stomach for some time. The doctors were amazed to see that the problem the mother came in with had disappeared. She went home without the operation.

Physical problems that have taken longer to manifest in the body will also take longer to heal. Broken bones obviously have to be set before being treated with Reiki. But the healing process will speed up tremendously with the input of Reiki.

I personally experienced this when I broke my elbow in three places a few years ago. The arm became as swollen as a football. It was too swollen to operate on and even to cast. I constantly did Reiki on it with my other hand. Because of this, the healing process happened much more quickly than normal. I also regained total mobility and had no pain after the healing had taken place.

Reiki for Children and in Pregnancy

Children usually love Reiki and respond quite quickly. If their parents have the Reiki initiations it becomes very natural for them to ask for Reiki if they have a headache or a stomach upset. The treatments become much more informal and shorter because children get restless lying still for a long time. They also tend to become quite hot during a treatment.

A good way is to do a spot treatment on the aching part. Another good way is having the child on your lap reading a story with one hand on their tummy.

It is also great to give pregnant women Reiki for all the tension they get carrying around the extra weight. The baby in the womb also benefits greatly.

My editor, Diana, treated her sister who was having some pain and tiredness in late pregnancy. As soon as she put her hands on her sister's leg, they both felt the baby moving around inside the womb.

I have initiated many pregnant women with Reiki so they were able to communicate with their unborn child in yet another way.

There is really no contraindication for treating with Reiki as long as the patient is willing to take responsibility for his or her reactions. Nobody can promise that a healing will occur. Only by trying can you see how a person responds.

Dying with the Support of Reiki

There are people who have been cured from cancer and other fatal diseases by Reiki and those for whom the Reiki has not worked on a physical level. But because Reiki is a spiritual energy, it can reconnect people to their spiritual selves, and help them to accept their transition. Reiki can also help with the pain and fear of dying.

I once treated a friend in the US who was dying of cancer. I used to treat her every other night or as often as she wanted, so she could go to sleep. I would just sit holding her feet, since it would hurt too much if I had my hands on the tumour. We chatted or watched television and I would sneak out after she had drifted into sleep. It felt very intimate and natural.

In Lyon, France, where I go regularly, I taught Reiki to a nurse, Isabelle. Through word of mouth, other nurses heard about it and came for initiations. Now, in the hospital where they work, the nurses have permission to use Reiki in the special ward for dying patients. The patients can now ask for a nurse who knows Reiki to sit with them.

As you can see, there is not a single situation in life where you cannot bring in the connection of Reiki. Experiences can range from a formal treatment to a friendly exchange or a rescue situation.

Many people, after experiencing the benefits of a Reiki session, want to learn it.

How do you do that? How do you get those 'magical hands'?

SEVEN

FIRST DEGREE
Reiki

First degree Reiki, which is hands-on healing, is normally taught in a workshop consisting of four two-hour sessions. The format is still pretty much the same as Takata used to do, except that she did the four sessions over four separate days. The group is normally quite small, up to twelve people. No previous knowledge is required. Many people have had experiences of Reiki treatments but this is not necessary.

As Reiki is an oral tradition, I start by telling the story of how I came to learn Reiki. While telling my story, I may touch on many things that the students will go through or feel themselves. I also talk about subtle energy in general but it really is not a metaphysical lecture. I am trying to convey an experience. Students with pencils and big notepads will be disappointed. In fact, Takata would not allow note taking or tape-recording in her classes. I understand why: when people write notes, their understanding is that the knowledge is apart from them, in the notebook. With Reiki, *they* are the book. The initiations will open up *their* intuition and inner knowing. It does not really matter if people remember what I talk about or not.

I continue to talk about my teacher, Wanja, and the stories about the Grand Masters, Usui, Hayashi and Takata. Then, if people do not have any questions, it is time for the first initiation.

Initiation

When giving the Reiki workshops I have a small room set aside for the initiations. I put the pictures of the Grand Masters, a candle and a flower on a table as a focus. I love to look at their smiling faces and the peace they emit. But if students think that this is a kind of mystical ceremony, I can do the initiation as well without any pictures.

I only need a chair for the student to sit on. I initiate the students one at a time. Takata sometimes used to initiate a few students at a time but I prefer to have a private moment with each student. Some students have strong emotional or spiritual experiences of the initiations. Others might want to say something in confidence.

The initiations are, as I have described before, to 'link up' the student as a Reiki channel. It is done with touch and silent mantras from the Reiki Master, while the students have their eyes closed and their hands folded in a praying position. There are four initiations for the first degree of Reiki. Each initiation only takes a couple of minutes and each one opens up the student on a deeper level. The last initiation closes the initiation process. Usually, one initiation will be experienced as stronger than the others.

The first degree initiations are to open up the heart, hand and top of the head chakras (energy centres) of the students so they can channel healing energies through their hands.

The first two initiations are given on the first day and the next two on the second day. It is important to have time between the initiations so people can 'digest the energy'. The initiations can give rise to a lot of powerful inner changes and transformations.

The timing of the initiations might vary according to the situation, but normally not more than two initiations should be given on one day. That would create too much heat in the body. It is also important that the students do not take drugs or drink alcohol during the workshop since the system is quite open and sensitive.

Demonstration of the Foundation Treatment

After an hour's break, we start the second session. I start to demonstrate the beginning of the foundation treatment, the positions on the head and the heart area. The students start practising on each other while I give the second initiations to the students, one by one.

During the third session, I go through the rest of the front positions and leave the back for the last session. The class practises while I continue to give initiations. Takata organized the workshop in this manner so that it would be easy to assimilate the information.

Before I go into more detail about the foundation treatment and positions of the hands, I want to stress again that without the initiations, the positions of the hands are pointless.

Hand Positions

Front positions

With the first hand position you cover the patient's eyes with the palms on the forehead and the fingers pointing down towards the jaw. There are two things going on here: the heat from the hands relaxes muscle tension in and around the eyes, but on a deeper level the subtle energy penetrates into the mind and calms down the thought process. Sometimes you can feel the thoughts like butterflies in your hands. The patient normally closes his eyes at this point and goes into a deep relaxation. This area is also good for treating sinus problems and strengthening the pituitary gland. Of course at the same time, as has been explained before, the patient automatically pulls the energy to the area in the body where it is needed. This area usually gets very hot. When the heat subsides it is time to move to the next position.

The second hand position is on the temples. The positions are not exact points as they are in acupuncture. I have seen this position differ quite a lot between Masters initiated by Takata. As in all positions, the fingers are held together without being tight, to concentrate the energy.

For the third position, you gently roll the head in your hands, so your hands end up under the patient's head, with the fingertips in the neck crease. All the three head positions are good for headaches and for bringing heat downwards from the head. Having the head cradled in this manner can feel very safe for the patient. The position can also be quite powerful. This is where the head meets the neck and the spine on a physical level. There can be a lot of muscular tension here that affects the whole body mechanism. On a subtle level, all the main chakras are situated in line with the spine. I usually hold this position for quite some time.

The fourth hand position covers the heart area. Wanja used to do this position from above the head of the patient. I find this too much of a stretch for my arms, so I do it from the side as I saw Mary McFadyon do, another of Takata's original Masters. On a physical level this position is good for asthma, bronchitis, etc. Sometimes you can feel old, cold, stuck energy leaving like a wind over the hands. There can also be a muscular tightness that usually corresponds emotionally to a closed heart or emotional pain. As this area opens up with the Reiki, it is usually accompanied by an emotional release.

The fifth hand position is on the stomach and spleen on the left side of the body. This position helps the digestion. Takata used to say that people treat their stomachs as garbage cans – they are not really conscious about what they eat.

The sixth hand position is on the opposite side of the body covering the liver. There can be a sense of fullness and heat in this position, especially if the patient has a liver problem. On an emotional level it corresponds to anger. One time I had a patient with quite a hot liver. I just said casually, 'Sometimes heat in the liver area corresponds to anger.' He jumped up to sitting position while shouting, 'I AM NOT ANGRY!' The next day he came back and told me that he had just read in an article that irritation was the same thing as anger. Maybe he was a little irritated, he confessed.

The seventh hand position covers the transverse colon, roughly level with the belly button. With the eighth position you put the hands in a V-shape over the ovaries on women – one hand on each ovary. It usually gets very hot in this position. This placement is good for period pain and cramping. Prostate problems are treated from the sacrum area.

Back positions

As the patient is turning over, you start by locating the spine. With parallel hands you work on each side of the spine. I usually start with the right shoulder first. This is where a lot of mental trauma is stored.

I continue with the left shoulder, the second position on the back, where more physical problems are stored. In general, shoulders have a lot to do with responsibility. We use a lot of expressions that mirror this fact: 'a chip on the shoulder', 'carry the world on your shoulders', etc.

The third and fourth positions are underneath the first two and cover the back of the lungs.

The fifth position is on the kidneys with one hand on each kidney. Roughly, they are located just above the waist. On an emotional level they are connected to fear. Often they can feel quite cold. You stay in this position until they have warmed up a bit and feel balanced with one another.

For the sixth position, you slide down the hands under the waist to cover the lumbar region or the lower back. A lot of people suffer from muscular tension here. Menstruating women often feel quite achy in this area.

The seventh position is on the sacrum area at the bottom of the spine. A position, as I said before, which is especially beneficial for men's prostate problems.

To finish off, you put one hand up to the top of the spine and keep the other on the sacrum. By this time at the end of the treatment, the spine should feel quite open and you should feel a pulsation between your hands.

To ground the patient and make her come back to her physical body you end the treatment with an energy stroke. Use the index and middle finger of one hand with the other hand on top as a weight and you run your fingers down each side of the spine in a downward stroke.

I have seen some variation in the hand positions used by different Masters initiated by Takata. At one point, I heard that she started her treatments on the digestive organs – the stomach/spleen and the liver – which shows the importance Takata placed on digestion. That, and the fact that she talked about organs and the emotions linked to them, shows the original strong connection of Reiki to oriental medicine.

It can be interesting to listen to what people talk about when you have your hands on different parts of the body. One woman to whom I was giving Reiki responded emotionally as if I had pressed a button on each position in which I was putting my hands. On the heart area she started crying. When I moved my hands to her liver, she started talking about the anger that she felt towards her work colleagues. Her response when I had my hands on her shoulders was to talk about how stressed she was about everything she had to do – including writing a thesis. On the kidney area she got into her fear and worry about her son becoming a punk.

Normally the legs and arms are not included in the foundation treatment unless the patient has a particular problem in that area or is extremely ungrounded. The Reiki will flow down anyway to the limbs. People often have tingling sensations there without any touch from the practitioner.

The amount of time spent in each position depends on the sensation in the practitioner's hands.

When there is a kind of stillness and not much is happening, it is time to move.

Sensation in the Hands

In the beginning when I did not feel much at all, I was extremely careful about dividing the one hour treatment time between the 16 positions. But as I started feeling more and more, it became very natural to feel how much time I should spend in each position. Actually, I completely stopped thinking about it. The hands started moving by themselves. There is a strong connection between the heart and the hands. As the heart opens up through Reiki, the hands know what to do, and there is no need for interference from the mind.

Sometimes the hands seem to get stuck in one position. There is a feeling of them being glued to the surface. This is a sign that the patient needs a lot of energy in this area. If your hand gets hot, there is too much activity in the area. You should stay until the heat has subsided. With cold it is the opposite – not enough energy or old, stagnant energy. The place needs to be warmed.

If there is pain in the area, sometimes you will feel pain in your hands. The more serious the pain is, the higher up the arms you will feel the pain. As you continue to treat the patient, the pain will subside.

When you get a tingly sensation in your hands, it means that some kind of release is occurring. Once, at the beginning of my Reiki practice, I was treating a woman and I felt a kind of tingling in a lot of places. I was quite pleased with the effectiveness of Reiki. The woman, however, had just three treatments. She told me that Reiki worked too well. She could not cope with all the 'stuff' that the Reiki brought up for her, she did not want to be that conscious!

At times you can feel something like an electric shock going up your arm. That is also some kind of dramatic release. There can be a lot of variation in how you perceive things, but the general rule is that you stay in an area as long as you sense that something is happening.

Sensations in the Body

When I had been practising for some time, I started to pick up what was happening in the patient in my own body. The sensation would stop when I took my hands off the patient. When I put my hands on the patient's head I could feel exactly where the energy was going, what was blocked, and the emotional state of the patient. I will give an example of this.

The Woman Who Could Not Cry

Diane came to me for Reiki treatments because she used to get styes in her eyes. As soon as I put my hands on Diane I felt enveloped in a cloud of sadness and I felt a deep pain in her heart. The sensation was so strong that I actually started to cry myself. It was a bit like when you cry when you see a sad movie. You know that it is not really your sadness. I could not help but say something like, 'Where does all this pain come from?' Diane felt very support-ed that somebody could acknowledge and feel the hurt that she was carrying with her all the time. It was the fact that she could not cry when she was feeling emotional that produced the styes.

With the Reiki the styes disappeared and she felt much better inside. Every time I see her now she wants me to put my hands on her to feel if any pain is left in her heart.

Finally, I want to make it clear that the Reiki does not get stronger because the practitioner feels more sensations. It just makes the treatment more interesting.

Receiving Information While Giving a Treatment

While giving a Reiki treatment you are in a heightened intuitive space because of the link-up to higher energies while you are channelling. You might get flashes of intuitive knowledge about the patient and her condition or changes that would improve her health. This can come in the form of phrases in your head, seeing images or just 'knowing'.

Once I treated a patient going through a difficult phase in his marriage. The phrase 'head and heart' kept repeating itself in my head. I realized his problem was a total disconnection between his mind and his emotions. This fact was totally supported by his wife, who complained about his way of rationalizing everything.

This kind of intuition has to be treated with delicacy – Reiki is not an encounter therapy, in which you tell people what is wrong with them and what they should do about it. It is much more valuable to give space for people to come to their own realizations.

One way to transmit this kind of information, if you feel it is useful knowledge for the patient, is to say, 'I have a sense or a feeling of ...,' and to give the patient the option to reject or accept what you have to say.

A method Wanja uses is a bit like what Miss Marple does in Agatha Christie mystery novels. She talks about somebody she knows whose case is similar to that of the patient. The patient then cannot go into reaction or denial, because nothing is mentioned about her. Unconsciously, she will identify herself with the person in the story and will receive the message. It is a great non-confrontational method.

Self-treatment

As Reiki is regarded as a spiritual practice and not just a healing method, people often ask what the practice is: it is to do treatments on yourself and others. It is while channelling Reiki that you are in contact with higher energies and the purification of your body-mind-emotions is accelerated.

Takata always stressed the importance of starting the healing process with yourself and working organically outwards to your family and friends.

In the beginning when I just learned Reiki, I did not do much self-treatment. I could not feel the energy on myself in the same way as when I treated others. I also had trouble believing that anything could happen when I put my hands on myself. Only when I became more sensitive and I could feel the energy sizzling around my body when I treated myself, did I become convinced.

Now I start every day with a self-treatment in bed for half an hour to an hour to link myself up to the energy source. It is a bit like a meditation and it is also a bit like an internal scanning of the body – to find what is blocked and what needs a bit of tuning. After eating, I put my hands on my stomach and liver to help the digestion. This is also part of a Qi Gong exercise, a Chinese energy system for healing. Going to sleep, I always have my hands on my heart, which is a very calming and nourishing position. While watching television you can always have your hands somewhere on your body, since hands-on Reiki works automatically without any intention on your part.

Because I now find self-treatment extremely important, I allow at least half an hour of the workshop to teach this practice. All the students line up like sardines on mattresses on the floor treating themselves by putting their hands on the positions on the front of the body.

The positions are basically the same as when you treat somebody else. You cannot comfortably treat the back, except the kidneys or lower back, which is done best in a sitting or standing position. Since the energy goes right through from the front, this is no problem. I usually add the position of the hands under the armpits to strengthen the immune system. It is good for women to give Reiki to their breasts to cut the accumulation of stagnant energy and prevent the formation of lumps. Of course, people can add any position they can comfortably reach!

It is important to understand that you do not have to go through the whole sequence of hand positions for self-treatment at once but can choose what is appropriate at any given time.

Just after I finished writing this, I went down to the kitchen to have some soup. Somehow I managed to drop the boiling soup on my arm instead of into my mouth. After rinsing the arm in cold water – on with the 'magical' Reiki hands. This reminds me to add that self treatment is absolutely brilliant in any kind of accident – I am fine now, with absolutely no pain!

Experiences and Reactions During the Workshop

It is very gratifying to see the transformations that students go through from the first day of the workshop to the second. As a teacher, the power of Reiki never stops amazing me. At the beginning of the first day people might be tense and a bit doubtful. The second day all tensions seem to have melted away. There is a glow in people's faces and they all look much younger.

Every group has its own rhythm and way of working. Sometimes there is almost complete silence with just a little whispering when people change positions. At other times there is a lot of giggling and almost a party feeling in the air.

At the end of the workshop people are so relaxed that they have a hard time moving. I especially remember a workshop I gave when I lived in Totnes in Devon. As we finished, we were sitting in a circle and nobody seemed to want to move. The energy in the room was so nice and peaceful that no one wanted to detach themselves from it. Slowly, everybody just keeled over and fell asleep! I crawled into my bed thinking that if everybody was going to stay over, at least I would sleep in my bed. An hour later everybody woke up and went home.

We start the second day with a session sharing about each individual's healing reaction to the initiations. I refer the reader back to

Chapter three. Because everybody in the class has different reactions, it is a good way of seeing how personally and differently people can react. It is important that the students understand the concept of healing crises and that they can see a clearing out experience in a positive light, both for themselves and for the patients they are going to treat.

The healing experiences from the initiations happen on four levels – spiritual, mental, emotional and physical – in the same way that a treatment works. The difference is that the energy of the initiations is much more powerful and transforming on a very deep personal level. The energy of a treatment will keep moving for 24 hours while the energy from the initiations takes two to three months to settle. Another difference is that you can lose the benefit of a treatment if you do not change the underlying factors that caused the problem in the first place, whereas the initiations always stay with you. They are permanent whatever you do.

I will give some examples of memorable healing reactions on different levels.

A Total Physical Cleanout

A woman in a workshop I held in France appeared very tense. After the first initiation, she started to feel sick. She began to throw up at the same time as having diarrhoea. As a matter of fact, she spent most of the workshop in and out of the bathroom. She was too ill to drive her car home so we had to call a taxi for her. As well as feeling sorry for her, I was a little worried that she would not be back for the second day. I had to give her the two last initiations, as it is important to go through the whole process, especially the last closing down initiation.

The next day she came back totally transformed with a big smile on her face. She told us that she felt great! She had been suffering from digestive problems and tension in the stomach area for many, many years.

An Anxiety Attack

A woman who suffered from anxiety attacks after having been raped came to me for Reiki treatments. I gave her a Reiki session while she was talking about her ordeal. She felt much better afterwards and I suggested that she take the Reiki initiations. She could then treat herself, if she had an attack, and calm herself.

During the first morning of the workshop she started to have a panic attack. I put my hands on her heart and I could feel her energy rising and her whole chest becoming tight. As I kept talking with my hands on her, I could slowly feel the tension subside and she started to breathe normally again.

When I talked to her shortly after the Reiki workshop, she told me that she had not had any more anxiety attacks.

Mental Reprogramming – Changes of Habits

Changes on a mental level are more subtle to perceive and seem to happen over a long period after the initiations. Eva, a friend of mine, wanted to learn Reiki in order to quit smoking. I told her that I could not guarantee anything, but if she really wanted to stop smoking,

Reiki would certainly help her. So much was happening during the Reiki workshop for Eva that we both forgot the smoking.

Later, when I remembered, I asked her about her smoking habit. Eva said that she had cut down her daily consumption to half without thinking about it.

Reiki helps to balance the whole system. As we open up to Reiki we get more sensitive and more in contact with what we do to ourselves. We can sense how unnatural it is to overload our systems with too much or the wrong kind of food, alcohol and drugs. Reiki also fills the spiritual emptiness or disconnection that often is at the base of the addiction.

One of my students, Migi, gives Reiki to many people with drug problems. As they get better they usually end up learning Reiki themselves from me. I have watched tremendous changes take place – not just quitting drugs but complete changes in lifestyle.

From Heroin to Reiki

Andrea is a woman who has been living in a drug environment since her teens and injecting heroin for thirteen years. She started to receive Reiki from Migi on a regular basis. Migi used to phone me for support since, at times, Andrea was in a very poor condition. There were times when she was totally cold. When she started to feel stronger but was still on heroin, Andrea came to me for the Reiki initiations. Her willingness to change convinced me to teach her. She was a lovely warm person with an artistic side. As she was feeling better with the Reiki, she started to channel her creativity into a jewellery making course. Her recovery has had its ups and downs, but she is moving in the right direction.

When Andrea's husband was dying of AIDS, the Reiki was able to support him, and her, through his transition. The support of the Reiki community was also around her during this difficult time. Her husband's last wish was for Andrea to quit heroin for good. With the money that he left her, Andrea decided to take the second degree Reiki initiation. The power of the second degree and the daily mental healings that Andrea had learned helped her in her struggle to combat the fear of living without drugs.

Also, the spiritual feeling of the second degree Reiki energy gave her the same 'high' as drugs but without the drawbacks and physical disintegration. This was the only thing she found that was equivalent to the feeling of being on drugs and made her realize for the first time that she could live without them.

Five months ago, Andrea met her spiritual teacher and started to practise yoga. At that time Andrea stopped taking drugs. She had a few relapses but is now totally clean. Andrea now wants to go back to her family to heal deep old wounds and move forward.

Spiritual Experiences

The strongest spiritual experience people usually have comes during the initiations themselves, because that is where the link-up to a higher power takes place. This is an experience that is hard to put into words. There can be a sense of connecting to the divine energy, a sense of this energy streaming down into the student. Some people see light or brilliant colours. One of my students had a vision of her spiritual teacher. A feeling of the heart opening – it can be a very emotional moment.

There often is a sense of feeling high or 'blissed out'. I had a student who could not stop laughing. He kept laughing all night long after the first initiations and felt high with a sense of extreme wellbeing for about 14 days after the workshop. Another woman, a friend of mine, who also felt this kind of high asked me, 'Does everybody go religious on you?' A friend who walked her home after the workshop said that she was walking in the middle of the road singing at full volume.

Perceptions also seems to change. Colours are more clear and vibrant. There is love in the air!

You might ask yourself, so, if this is first degree Reiki, what does the second degree Reiki bring? When can I learn it?

EIGHT

SECOND DEGREE
Reiki

People who have learned first degree Reiki and feel enthusiastic about it usually continue and learn the second degree Reiki. As a guideline, it is good to wait a couple of months for the reactions of the first degree's initiations to settle. Some people wait years before they go on to the next step, and others are happy with just the first degree. It is a personal choice.

If a person can handle the energy, it is possible to learn second degree Reiki right after the first degree. There are situations where this is more practical. Takata sometimes taught one degree right after the other. This happened in Canada where people had waited for her to come for a long time and had travelled long distances. Wanja had to teach me second degree Reiki immediately after the first degree, because not all the deer in the ashram would stand still for a hands-on treatment.

So what is second degree Reiki?

With second degree Reiki you learn to send distant healing, to work on a mental level to solve problems with people and situations, to clear spaces and project wishes. You can also learn how to connect and communicate with animals and nature.

The way of working is with symbols. It also involves one more initiation. Another benefit of taking the second degree Reiki is that the power of the hands on healing is doubled. The second degree initiation also continues to deepen the inner personal transformations that started with the first degree Reiki.

Takata used to say that the first degree is like driving a car slowly at 30 miles an hour and taking in the landscape. You can also drive at 80 miles an hour to get to the same point. Distant healing is like when you step on the pedal and you get to the same place faster.

Second Degree Workshop

The format of the second degree workshop is normally two two-hour sessions on successive days. We always start by sharing experiences people have had while practising the first degree hands-on Reiki. It is really by using the Reiki on themselves, family members and friends that people become convinced that Reiki works.

I also answer any questions that have come up about hands-on healing and try to explain unusual experiences that people might have had. I want to be sure that there are no uncertainties left about the first degree Reiki before we go to the next level.

The Symbols

On the first day we go through the symbols that are used for sending and projecting energy. These symbols should be given to you by a Reiki Master in combination with the second degree initiation. They are secret and sacred and should be treated with respect. The paper they are written on while practising should not be thrown in a waste basket, but burned after having been learned by heart. The symbols in themselves carry a certain energy even without the initiations. I will give an example of this.

A man came back on the second day of the second degree workshop a bit puzzled. He said that when he came home after the first day he had a very strong emotional reaction. He was crying and trembling but he could not understand why, since in his words, 'we had not done anything'. I had to explain that his experiences came from drawing the symbols. The names of the symbols also carry energy, they function as mantras – holy sounds.

The power of the second degree is the combination of the drawing of the symbols, the sounds of their names and the initiation. You could say that the initiation activates the symbols.

After the first day, the students take their copies of the symbols with them as homework to be learned by heart. Many students feel anxious that they will forget the symbols or not be able to remember them completely accurately. They just have to think back to when they learned the alphabet. In the beginning everybody carefully copied the teacher. Later, people developed all kinds of writing styles, but the letters still meant the same thing. It is the same thing with the symbols. The intention behind them is the important thing as long as they are recognizable.

It seems that Takata drew the symbols a little differently at times. I have compared the symbols that Takata gave Wanja with the way other Masters initiated by Takata draw them and there are slight variations.

Initiation and Practice

The second day we start practising after the students have been initiated. There is only one initiation for the second degree, but it is a bit more elaborate than the initiations for the first degree.

As with the hands-on healing, we start the healing by working on each person's own issues. We sit in a circle and everybody in turn chooses something to work on with the group. Each person can choose between having a distant Reiki treatment, a distant mental Reiki working on some personal problematic situation, or a wish. We usually end by communicating with trees or something in nature.

Since it can be difficult to believe that sending energy in this way really works, it is good to start sending to the people who are present. In this way you get immediate feedback.

I remember being a bit of a 'doubting Thomas' myself, when I had just learned distant healing. To see if it would work, I put a friend with a headache in a corner of a room and started to send him some Reiki. While sending energy I kept asking, 'How does it feel now? How is your head?' Seeing for myself that his headache disappeared little by little was the proof I needed. I think a bit of scepticism is quite healthy.

The advantage of sending energy in a group, apart from it being stronger, is that people can compare the sensations they pick up and feel.

Picking up the Information

When you are sending Reiki, either a distant healing or a mental healing, you put the hands up in front of you so you can sense the energy being pulled through you and out of the hands. The more the person or the situation needs, the more Reiki will be pulled through you. It can feel like heat, tingling or vibration in the hands. As you keep practising, you will start picking up emotional states or physical pain of the person or situation on whom or which you are working. Sometimes you can get intuitive information or see pictures in your mind.

We try not to stop the flow of intuition by judging what is wrong or right, but it is important not to treat this information as fact. As with the hands-on Reiki, you are receiving a treatment at the same time as you are giving one. What you pick up can have something to do with your own personal 'stuff'. The more you practise, the more your intuition will grow and become clearer and clearer. Of course, as with hands-on healing, Reiki works regardless of what you feel.

Another important issue is that, of course, whatever information that people pick up is confidential.

The second degree needs a little more focus than the first degree, so we usually keep our eyes closed while we are sending distant Reiki.

Distant Healing

When sending distant healing, the actual distance is of no importance. There is no difference in the procedure for sending distant healing to a person in the same room or in another country. Sometimes it is more convenient to do distant healing than hands-on, even if you are in the same place, for example in a car.

Once I was in a taxi returning to New York from a meditation retreat. At the beginning of the two-hour journey the taxi driver complained about pains in his back and groin. I said I would try to do something about it. As we kept talking I was sending him distant Reiki. Just outside New York, I asked him how he was feeling, if he still was in pain. He was quite taken aback when he realised that his pain had disappeared. He said that if he had not worked for a company, he would have given me the ride for free.

Another advantage of distant healing is that because it is much more powerful than the hands-on healing, you only have to do up to 20 minutes instead of an hour. Sometimes not even that much time is needed, if there is no 'pull' in the hands and the energy feels quite settled.

Often it is practical to combine the first degree with the second degree Reiki. If, for example, it is difficult for a patient to come three or four days in a row for hands-on treatments, you can send a distant treatment instead.

There is no need to ask permission from the person to whom you send distant healing. You are just sending unconditional love. Who would refuse? There is also no need for the person receiving the Reiki to lie down or even to know the time when it is happening, though this might be interesting from a scientific point of view.

Distant Group Healing

Often people want to learn distant healing because they have a family member with some physical problem living in another city or even in another country, and they want to help. There was a woman in a second degree workshop who wanted to learn distant healing because her mother, who lived elsewhere, had a frozen shoulder. We were quite a big group sending the mother healing while practising. Straightaway afterwards we phoned the mother. She told us that she was having a shower at the exact time as we were sending her healing. Suddenly she noticed that she could stretch up the arm that was hardly movable before!

Not every case has such a dramatic effect after just one distant Reiki treatment, but it is a great way to keep in contact with friends and family. I always start the day by sending some energy to my mother in Sweden. There is no limit to how often you can do a distant treatment. You can keep sending Reiki every day for serious problems. The more people there are working together on one person, the stronger the healing effect. Often my Reiki students call to ask me to send some Reiki to them or to their friends in need. It feels like a great form of meditation, you can help somebody and at the same time be in contact with the higher power, the source.

The latest example I have of this kind of group effort is the mother of one of my students, who had two brain haemorrhages. A whole group of Sue's Reiki friends keep sending healing to her mother, who now seems much better and well on the way to a full recovery. She came out of her coma within 48 hours and was walking and talking within five weeks. The doctors and surgeons could not explain it. She was critically ill, had had two bleeds in her brain and, they believed, she would not even wake up for two weeks – if at all. Sue believes it is a total miracle.

It is also good in these cases to send healing to the people around the sick person as they go through a lot of worry and heartache.

What if a Person Does Not Want to be Healed?

Once I was asked in a second degree workshop if we could send some healing to a woman who lived in the same house as one of my students and was suffering from cancer. She had refused conventional treatment because she did not believe in it. The problem was that she was not doing much in the form of alternative treatment either. The people in the house living with her were terribly worried for her.

As we put up our hands, I felt something I have never felt before or since. It felt like hitting a brick wall; no energy went through it. Yet we knew that she needed it. Everybody in the group felt the same thing. The only thing I could think of was the fact that she had not asked for the healing herself. Maybe she wanted to go? So instead of sending Reiki to her, we started sending healing to all the other people in the house. Here it felt like a great need, and as if the energy was being sucked out of our hands.

I think that sometimes, as healers, we want to heal everybody and everything and feel disappointed when this is not happening. It is important to have a detached attitude. We do what we can, but the result is not up to us. Maybe the physical tissues are too damaged or maybe it is just time for the person to leave.

Wanja once told me the story of a dog with cancer that she healed with Reiki. The next day he ran in front of a car and died. It was his time.

Mental Healing

When sending mental healing you add a symbol that works as a key to open up your mind to another person's mind or to a situation. You can also use this symbol to communicate with animals and nature, clear spaces or situations in the past or future and project wishes. The use of this symbol is very versatile as you can see.

When projecting specific energy to a person in this way, you need the person's permission. You also need to be very focused, because everything you think enters into the other person. It is a reprogramming for mental problems so you need to send positive

83

affirmations or images. Because this kind of healing is much stronger than just distant healing, you only need to send for ten minutes.

I will make the process clearer by giving an example. If a person wants help for his depression, you want to send some positive emotion. If you decide to send joy, you have to visualize the person in a happy situation, repeat affirmations about the person being joyful or create uplifting images from nature. If your mind wavers you should stop.

Divine Order: Another Dimension of Spiritual Healing

There is another way of sending mental healing in which you do not have to visualize the solution to the problem. You just state the problem and add the phrase 'Divine Order' to the mental symbol. This is more like a prayer, you are sending the problem to the higher mind instead of manipulating the energy yourself. 'Divine Order' also means that it will only happen if it is in the divine plan, if it is good for the person. When you send mental healing in this way, once again you do not need to ask permission.

I much prefer this way of working. This is also the way to work with problem situations and wishes.

The only time I use the mental key without 'Divine Order' is when I want to communicate directly with animals, plants and nature. I open the direct channels. I can send information but I can also stay open and receive at the same time.

I will give some example of different uses of mental Reiki, starting with communication with animals.

Monkeys in Kenya

For a few years I went to Kenya to teach Reiki at the invitation of a healing society in Nairobi. I stayed and held most workshops in a beautiful country home in Limuru. In the garden there were some tree circles of eucalyptus with especially strong energy, where we did our second degree practice. We were quite a big group sitting inside the circle as old students came to join us.

We saw some monkeys playing far away in the tree tops. I suggested that we send them a mental message to come closer so we could look at them. With our hands up in the air using the mental key we started to project this message. We had hardly begun before one of the big monkeys started to swing from tree to tree getting closer to where we were sitting. He stopped in one of the trees above our heads and started to throw branches down on us. After a while he got tired and left. We then continued sending for the second monkey. He came over and repeated the first monkey's antics. It was quite mind boggling!

How to Become a Nice Cat

A friend of mine, Rita, was afraid of cats. She was visiting friends who had warned her about their vicious cat. One evening the cat came into Rita's bedroom and started staring at her. She was petrified. She sat up in her bed but did not dare to move out of the bed in case the cat attacked her. As she knew Reiki, she started to tell the cat, while sending mental Reiki, how a nice cat behaves – being fluffy and soft, purring and friendly, sitting in people's laps, etc. The cat went through a metamorphosis, she kept following Rita around stroking herself on her legs. The cat's owners could not believe what had happened to their monster. After a couple of months the cat went back to some of her old bad habits. She probably needed a little more reminding.

This makes me think of another cat story.

The Cat in Love with the Lady Cat Across the Road

A cat owner wanted the second degree group to send mental Reiki to her cat to stay in her garden. She was afraid the cat would be run over when crossing the street. As I started sending, I got images of the cat and the feeling that he received the message, but was not really interested in following the advice. I also saw vague images of another cat with whom our cat seemed infatuated.

The rest of the group came to the same conclusion. The owner then agreed that she also thought there was a bit of romancing behind her cat's disappearances. So there is a free will even in the cat world.

Communicate with
Trees and Nature

A good way to replenish your energy is to connect to trees, rivers, mountains, oceans and even planets. Everything has its own energy pattern so you can just tune into what you need at the moment. Trees are especially good if you feel ungrounded. With their roots in the ground, vertical trunk and crown in the sky, it feels like having an Alexander lesson in which your spine lengthens and you open up to the world from a very supported position. Every tree feels a little different. It is good to choose a strong, healthy-looking tree. In the winter it is good to choose an evergreen because trees without leaves are drawn into themselves and feel like sleeping.

To connect to oceans feels expanding and very relaxing; volcanoes with all that inner activity are good for digestion. It is a great way to play around and make your own discoveries.

Ghostbusting

Another way you can use mental healing is to clear bad energies from spaces. When I moved into a house in London with some friends, the room that I was allotted had terrible energy. The person who had lived there before had been very emotionally disturbed. The room felt cold and very unsettled. I started clearing the space before I even moved in, with incense and by playing a tape of continuous mantra music. I also did a lot of mental Reiki to clear out any subtle garbage clinging to the room.

A room or place is not very different from a person. In the same way that a person can have negative memories and stagnant energy from the past, a room has subtle imprints of everything that has taken place there. The same thing goes, of course, for positive energy and experiences.

When the Chinese caretaker came to the house, being interested in Feng Shui, he was amazed at the energy transformation of the room. He later phoned me wanting me to come with him and our landlady to chase some bad spirits and energy away from an apartment that she was thinking of buying. I declined the offer, saying that it was not really my speciality. I promised, though, to send some positive energy there while practising second degree with one of my students.

As we started sending we both felt some kind of nauseating energy coming through from the flat. There was even a strong odour attached to it. It was the first time I had experienced that kind of thing. After a while it started to clear. Our Chinese landlady was most impressed and told me that the apartment had a very bad smell because it had been used as a dentist's surgery. She then wanted me to ghostbust her office from bad luck!

I have dropped this possible sideline. I prefer to strengthen the positive, instead of getting involved in negative things.

Following a Peruvian Shaman

A great way to work with the mental Reiki is to project wishes. Because you use the prefix 'Divine Order', you know that it will only happen if it is for your own good, if it is in the divine plan.

A woman to whom I was teaching second degree Reiki said she wanted to earn enough money to go to Peru and spend some time with her shaman teacher, Juan. As we were formulating the wish I just said spontaneously, 'Me too!' I had for some time been interested in the shamanic way of healing. When we put our hands up I could feel an incredible energy coming into the room. I just said aloud, 'What is this?' The woman answered that this was her teacher Juan. We sat with our hands up, pinned against the wall for about 45 minutes.

Some weeks later I happened to teach a few unusually big classes that left me with the exact amount of money I needed to go to Peru. I phoned a contact number in Brussels and found that there was only one place left in the group that was to work and travel with Juan. I was told to meet up with the group in a hotel in Lima on a certain date. I arrived at the hotel in the middle of the night. The next morning when coming down to the lobby, I saw a beautiful, very solid South American Indian, with long hair and a shining face, talking with some people. At first I thought it was a woman because of the softness of the gestures and posture. I was wrong – this was Juan.

I spent two incredible weeks in Juan's company while he, in accordance with his tradition, tried to scare the living daylights out of me – we crossed wild rivers, crawled in underground tunnels, climbed mountains and walked on the Inca pass where you almost die looking down into the deep abysses.

I learned about Pacha Mamma – Mother Earth – and our connection to her. I had incredible experiences with energy and I must say that I have never seen such a beautiful country, situated high up in the clouds.

Open up the Creative Flow

One of my students in Paris, a painter, always does mental Reiki in order to connect herself to her inner creativity and intuition. I do the exact same thing before sitting down in front of my computer to write this book.

For written tests and exams it is great to ask for clarity of mind and maybe also for a feeling of calm. People have asked me to send Reiki while they are delivering talks, and said they could feel the peacefulness of the energy descending on them.

Healing the Past

When dealing with energy there are no limits to time or space. The mental Reiki can also be used to go back in time and heal traumatic situations that occurred in childhood. I have worked in this way with a woman who was sexually abused. Some people who have experienced sexual abuse seem to be internally frozen in a state of fear. This is not just fear that comes from the initial abuse, but also fear of feeling in general, and sometimes an inability to access and express anger. Reiki can help to integrate and release these emotions.

The woman told me that Reiki has helped to shift things for her. Of course, this is a slow process and she also does other things to help heal her early wounds.

Healing Political Situations

Sometimes Reiki groups get together to send healing energy to more global and political situations.

During the Gulf War there were a lot of activities taking place on a subtle level, not just from Reiki groups, but from many meditation and healing groups all around the world. A lot of healing energy was sent to that situation.

If a person really understands the three symbols, they are like tools in a toolbox that can be used creatively in many different situations.

NINE

REIKI FOR ANIMALS
and Plants

I grew up in a home where everybody loved animals. My father was brought up in the country, and though we lived in a small town, we had a mini farm with cats, dogs, dwarf chickens and rabbits in our garden. Even though my father was not a vet but a biology teacher, people treated him a bit like Dr Dolittle. During the winter when it was cold and difficult for birds to survive, people would bring starving, half frozen and injured birds for him to care for at home. We all helped to feed and take care of the animals that were brought to us.

At one time we had an injured, aggressive swan in our hallway. Another time we had a baby owl in our basement, too young to fly, whom we fed with meatballs while wearing gloves for protection. We then had to teach him to fly before letting him go.

Having this kind of background and love for animals made me look upon Reiki as a great gift. Finally I had a tool for healing when animals were sick. It is not always enough to have a desire to help.

Different Ways to Treat Animals

If an animal is tame, the easiest way to give Reiki is hands-on healing. If possible, you put the hands on the injured part of the animal. If this is not convenient, put the hands anywhere you can since, as with people, the Reiki goes where it is needed. Animals, like children, tend to get very hot during a Reiki session, so the treatment tends to be shorter. If the heat of the Reiki makes an animal restless, you can just caress it. The lifting of the hands when stroking makes the treatment less intense and is a behaviour the animal is more used to and understands. The Reiki will come through anyway.

Putting the hands in the animal's drinking water to energize was a practice that Wanja and I used while healing the deer.

Another way of using water to intensify the treatment is to rinse a towel in water and put it on the animal with your hands on it while giving Reiki. As water conducts energy, it facilitates the flow of Reiki to the areas you cannot reach. This is especially practical for big animals such as cows or horses as it is difficult to put your hands all over their bodies. It is not necessary for smaller animals which you can hold in your hands.

For wild animals and when the animal is not present, distant Reiki is extremely convenient. Mental Reiki is great for communication and solving behavioural problems in animals. In the section below I will give experiences of using Reiki with animals.

Healing the Deer in the Ashram

After the deer were cured from foot-and-mouth disease, I used the Reiki in all kinds of emergency situations, especially during the mating season, when there was a lot of fighting between the male deer. I used to hear their antlers clashing in the night. Knowing that their fights might lead to death, I would sometimes run out and break up their fighting with a big stick.

The injuries resulting from their fighting would be ears hanging on by a thread, eyes bulging and small circular swellings from antler wounds all over their bodies. I used to clean the wounds with peroxide, put the gel of the aloe vera plants that grew in the garden on top and then do Reiki. The speed at which the wounds healed was quite amazing.

I especially remember a deer that had an antler poked into his eye. The eye was so swollen that it looked as if it was going to pop out of its socket. I kept feeding him carrots while putting my hand over his injured eye. After a couple of days the eye sunk into the socket with the cornea looking like a folded clear tape. The eye looked milky and opaque and seemed to have no sight. Meanwhile, a pocket of pus, big as a fist, was forming underneath the eye. I kept giving Reiki since I did not want the other eye to get infected too and leave him blind in both eyes.

I certainly had to learn not to be squeamish, as the pus started to pour out underneath the eye. After a week the swelling had leaked out, the eye came back to its normal position, the cornea stretched out again and the colour of the eye went back to normal. I realised that the deer could see with it again!

Have You Seen a Spotted Deer Pass By?

My worst nightmare was when the deer escaped from the deer park. It was very tricky to get them back in again – it took a lot of carrots and cajoling. If they felt in any way chased after, they would panic and run further away.

Somehow a beautiful deer, Gopal, got out of the deer compound and was running around loose in the ashram gardens. As people had been trying to be helpful and chase him back in, he was quite 'freaked out'. I found Gopal standing with his nostrils flaring and a wild look in his eyes close to the very high ashram wall. He looked at the trees on the other side, looked at me, then crashed into the wall, bounced back, and jumped again. My heart stood still as I watched him sail over the wall.

On the other side Gopal stopped to graze. As I came around the wall myself I lost sight of him. I kept asking people I met if they had seen a spotted deer pass by. In the end I did not have to ask, they just pointed in the direction of the village. Outside the village was a swamp, where I could see a big group of people gathered. Coming closer, I could see them surrounding Gopal who was lying unconscious covered in mud on the ground.

Gopal had been found swimming in the swamp and was dragged out to be rescued or eaten, I did not know which. I just threw myself on top of him in order to protect him. I remembered that Wanja had said that if you are a Reiki Master the healing comes out of your whole body and not just the hands. Lying in this position, I tried to organise a bull-cart or an ashram vehicle to come and get us.

After what seemed like eternity a van pulled up and we loaded the still seemingly lifeless deer. Back in the deer park I hosed Gopal down to remove all the mud and put him in a dark shed to recover from the shock. According to a book I read about deer farming, a deer, being a wild animal, can die from shock after being held down for more than ten minutes. I continued to give Gopal hands-on Reiki and he started to move a little the second day. But for several days he was not himself. He would lie beside me like a dog and not move while I was giving him Reiki, something he never would have allowed before. It took a week for him to stand on his legs and behave like a deer again.

Then he was up to new mischief – but that, again, is another story!

Healing Birds

While taking care of the deer in the ashram, I was also responsible for the peacocks. With them, I mostly used distant healing, since wild birds can also go into shock and die if held long against their will.

Only when birds have already been shocked by flying into a fan or a window have I used hands-on healing. With a few minutes of Reiki they often recover quite quickly.

With mental healing, you can work on mental and emotional problems the animals have. I once sent a lot of mental healing to a parrot called Sita who had both emotional and behavioural problems. She was a very shy and unhappy parrot who used to pick all her feathers off and chew on them. Sita had had a traumatic past. She had been shipped on a boat from South America to India, lost her mate and been put with another male parrot who used to pick on her.

I used mental healing, both using 'Divine Order' and direct communication, with Sita, talking to her out loud and in my mind, sending her love and reassurance and also trying to persuade her not to pick her feathers. I would sit in her large aviary while Sita was sitting on a branch in a corner, as far away from me as possible. While sending Reiki, I could sense the pain in her heart. The emotional states picked up from animals do not feel any different to those from humans.

As I kept working with her, I felt her heart open up slightly. This might be hard to believe but I can only say that that was how it felt. I started to feed her with food on a stick. Sita would come very reluctantly, grab the food and run away on her branches. She was quite a character and I grew very fond of her. In the mornings when I used to come, she would rush around and make a lot of noise. When I started sending Reiki she parked herself on a branch and looked intently at me. As the healing progressed, she half-closed her eyes and seemed to slide into something like a meditation.

Sita's caretaker and I encouraged her to take food from our hands by giving her less food in her bowl. I also used Reiki to build up a trusting relationship. She did become much tamer and seemed calmer. She still picked her feathers, but to a lesser degree. It is much easier to shift an emotional state than an addictive behaviour. Before I left, I taught Sita's caretaker Reiki so she could continue the work with Sita and help the other animals in her care.

A Baby Sea Lion

While teaching Reiki in California, I visited the Marine Mammal Centre in Marin County outside San Francisco. Here they rescue and take care of sea lions and seals who have been found sick or injured on the surrounding beaches. Many healers go there to work as volunteers and to do healing on the animals.

A baby sea lion named Mike had been found on a beach abandoned by his mother. Unfortunately the person who found him had wrapped him in a blanket and overheated his system causing some brain damage. Mike was extremely cute with dark eyes like a puppy, but he could not walk properly; his balance had been affected so he kept falling over.

I was sending distant healing to Mike together with another healer who used her own healing system. In addition to Mike's physical problems, we could both feel his emotional state, his sadness and longing for his mother. We both had tears in our eyes after the healing.

I was not able to visit the centre after that time, but I heard through friends who continued the healing sessions with Mike that he got completely well and was released into the ocean again.

Letting Go

My friend Edith, who brought me to the Marine Mammal Centre, had a beautiful Siberian Husky called Sheleili. The dog was very old and had a lot of physical problems, including cancer of the kidneys. Edith was extremely close to Sheleili and wanted me to do some Reiki on her. The thought of Sheleili dying was very upsetting to Edith.

As I settled into the healing session, I could sense Sheleili's tiredness, in fact it felt as if she was hardly in her body any longer. There was an enormous sense of peace surrounding her. She was ready to go as soon as Edith would let her. My work was not with the dog but with Edith. I spoke to my friend about her anxiety around losing Sheleili. We did some mental healing about her attachment. Shortly after that, Edith decided to put Sheleili to sleep instead of prolonging her suffering.

An Angry Cow with an Attitude

Takata taught Reiki to many farmers on Hawaii. One of the results is said to have been that their cows gave more milk and were happier in general.

Once on a meditation retreat I was asked to do some Reiki on a cow that was quite temperamental and created problems for her caretakers. The retreat was situated in upstate New York and took place in the middle of a snowy winter. I went out to the cowshed and found one of the cowhands and tried to explain to him what I was going to do. He looked puzzled but showed me to my patient who was standing in a field.

The cow looked quite mean so I decided I was better off with a fence between us. I found an old chair in the barn, sat down, put my gloved hands up in the air and started to do mental Reiki for the cow to become more sociable. It felt surreal sitting there in the winter landscape trying to influence this cow with an attitude. It was cold, too.

When the cow turned her back on me, I decided to continue this distant healing from a warmer place – like my hot bathtub.

For a few days I did distant mental healing on the cow from my living quarters. Later I went back to the cow to see how she was doing. Putting my hands up to send distant Reiki, still with a fence between us, she came up close to me pushing against my hands and wanting to be stroked. What a transformation!

Healing Horses

The first horse owner I taught Reiki to was a woman in New Mexico with 25 polo horses. She learned both first and second degree Reiki so she could care for the horses herself if they got any injuries while she was transporting them from New Mexico to California. She had no problems understanding the concept of mental and distant healing, since she felt that she already had a very strong telepathic connection with her horses.

This is something I come across frequently with animal lovers – because animals do not talk, the communication is already happening on another level. The health and the emotional state of an animal are often a reflection of the owner.

Once I was trying to get hold of my agent Susan and was sending some Reiki to that effect. I was also sending some Reiki for her horse who had some problems. To my surprise, they felt emotionally the same – in shock. Later, I heard that the horse had been injured running into a gate, and they were both suffering the same emotional impact.

Danny, a riding school teacher and Alexander teacher, was so impressed with the Reiki healing that a friend of mine did on one of his horses that he wanted to learn it himself. He later invited me to give a class for other people at his riding school. I always love to teach Reiki to people who love animals since animals have played such an important part in my life.

The kinds of problems Danny thinks Reiki has helped the horses with are: discomfort and pain, swellings, muscular strains, sprains and stress. He has also had success with colds and infections such as glandular swellings behind the ears. Fadie, a dog living at the riding school, has become a bit of a Reiki addict. He will get close to Danny and demand Reiki by putting forward the body part that he wants to be treated.

Animals Love Reiki

I had already noticed with the deer that animals enjoyed getting Reiki. They became tamer as I treated them and would come up to me more often for a nuzzle. If there are animals like cats and dogs around while I am giving a Reiki class or a treatment, they usually place themselves on top of the patient. Even when the patient has left, they choose to lie down on the energy imprint left behind.

I will never forget a 19-year-old cat named Marichan in San Francisco who had unusually large paws because she had an extra claw on each paw. Marichan was very much in tune with her owner Machan and when she saw her practising Reiki, she obviously felt invited to take part in the healing session that was under way in the living room. After taking one glance at us with our hands on a friend, she positioned herself with two paws on the ground and the other two firmly placed on the body on the floor. She refused to budge and we had to remove her paws when turning the patient.

Healing Trees and Plants

In the same way that animals like Reiki, so do plants. Reiki does not just go in a linear way from practitioner to patient. When Reiki is practised an energy field is created. A clairvoyant who watched me giving a Reiki session saw an orange cloud of energy coming out of my body as I started the session. After the Reiki treatment it took about five minutes for the cloud to vanish. This field of energy, or life force, makes plants grow healthier and in more abundance. You can always tell what is going on in a place by looking at the state of the plants.

The first time I did healing on plants was in the ashram in India. I was asked by one of the gardeners to give some healing to a few bushes that had been replanted. I thought he just wanted to be nice to me, knowing that I had just learned this new 'thing' – Reiki. As I put my hands on the stem of one of the bushes I did not expect anything particular but I was in for a surprise. I could actually feel the trembling and shock inside the bush. I was feeling the reality of the expression that a plant goes into shock when replanted.

Later I did a lot of distant healing on trees that had been replanted and they felt the same, only stronger.

Working on plants, you can cup your hands around them or touch their stems. You can also energize the water that you use for watering with Reiki. Holding seeds for a while in the hands before planting is another way of giving Reiki.

One of my students used to give her whole garden distant Reiki. It is just a question of being creative. Anything is possible!

TEN

LIVING WITH
Reiki

Once I had learnt Reiki it became part of my life. I naturally used it on others and on myself in all kinds of situations. When I came home from India and talked about my spiritual experiences there, people would respond and say that obviously meditation was good for me. But there was not much interest. With Reiki it was a different story. Everybody wanted Reiki treatments. I became very popular! With friends and family you can also give treatments quite casually. I usually sit behind my mother with my hands on her shoulders when she is watching television or have my hands on somebody's feet while having a conversation.

I have a friend called Melissa who had 'restless legs', a condition in which the legs become spastic during the night. While we lived in the same house, I often used to hold her feet while sitting and talking before going to sleep. On the evenings I did this, the legs would be calm all through the night.

When I became a Reiki Master, my first student was my 88-year-old mother. She does not treat anybody but uses Reiki on herself. It is a great gift to give to somebody. I have given Reiki sessions and initiations for birthdays and Christmas presents to the rest of my family – brothers, sister, sisters-in-law, brother-in-law and all the children. Reiki is a great thing to share!

I usually start my day by giving myself a Reiki treatment in bed while trying to remember my dreams. It is a great way to wake up! While having my bath, I usually send distant Reiki to some special people.

After eating, I hold my hands on the stomach and liver to help digestion. Going to sleep I have my hands on my heart – it is a very calming and comforting position and great for insomnia. I think Reiki should be like brushing your teeth – a good habit that is incorporated into your daily living.

There have also been special occasions when Reiki has helped me and others and brought a richness into my life.

Fear of the Dentist

When I was little I used to go to a dentist who did not like to use anaesthesia while he was drilling because it meant that the treatment would take longer. He used to say that it was not going to hurt. When it did, I totally lost faith and I developed a fear of dentists. I would dread my visits for months in advance. Even as I walked through the door, I would make him promise to give me an injection to kill the pain – just in case.

As an adult, I had less fear since I chose a dentist who actually listened to me. But my fear had submerged to an unconscious level. When I had too many instruments in my mouth, I would get an involuntary reflex, choke and spit them out. Apart from being uncomfortable for me, it was highly embarrassing and time-consuming.

It was some time after I learned Reiki that I realized I could put one hand on my chest while my dentist was working and give myself Reiki to stop these gagging reflexes. Without Reiki I could never have gone through with having my amalgam fillings removed and replaced with a less toxic material. I spent hours in a relatively calm state with my excellent Swedish dentist, who ended up taking the Reiki initiations himself.

I have also had the opportunity to assist a dentist in the US who specializes in root canal treatment by giving Reiki to nervous patients with very good results.

Curing Hangovers

In Sweden Midsummer's Night is celebrated all night long because of the light. One year I was invited to celebrate in a summer house on Väddö, an island outside Stockholm. It was a beautiful place but as the night proceeded people got more and more drunk. Since I had just left the ashram with its disciplined life, I wondered what on earth I was doing there and went to bed.

The next morning, many people suffered from hangovers. I offered to help somebody by giving Reiki outside on the grass lawn since it was a glorious sunny day. During the treatment other people became very curious and before I knew it I had a queue of prospective customers.

Not only did the Reiki help the hangovers but I discussed very deep issues with many people, which was completely the opposite to the more superficial interaction I had had the evening before. It was as if the Reiki cut through the more social communication to a level where things really mattered to a person.

I especially remember a woman who was pregnant and was considering having an abortion because the nuclear accident at Chernobyl had just occurred and she was afraid that the foetus might be damaged by radiation. A man was contemplating a total change in his life and career. I cannot remember all the personal stories, but I do remember being moved and amazed at everything that was going on inside the people at the party.

I was giving Reiki practically continuously from morning to evening that day. I had my hands on somebody in the bus going to the beach. On the beach, I gave somebody else a treatment. I remember the sounds of the waves and the feeling of sun on the skin, and sinking into an extremely profound meditation that was hard to get out of for both of us.

On the way back to Stockholm I was with a woman who insisted on learning Reiki before I left for Devon, England, the next morning. Before she went home at midnight, she had her first initiations and practice. At six o'clock the next morning, before going to work as a teacher for young children, she was back for her last initiations. She got her last-minute instructions as she helped me take my luggage to the bus for the boat to England. I was impressed with her dedication.

Learning how to Drive

Being dyslexic and not very technically orientated, I never thought I could learn how to drive a car. A couple of years ago, I thought that I would take it up as a hobby to see what would happen. Having gone through a number of teachers who were very agitated when I turned left instead of right, screamed at me and upset me, I talked about my problem to my acupuncturist, Lynn. Being a sensitive person herself, she had run into similar problems when she learned to drive.

Lynn told me that she had found a very caring and understanding woman driving instructor whom she could recommend. I started to have lessons from Jean who was everything my acupuncturist had told me she would be.

One damp London day while sitting in the car, I felt a restriction in my chest and I found it difficult to breathe. I recognized the feeling from people I had treated for asthma, so I turned to my driving teacher and asked her if she had asthma. Jean looked quite startled and asked me how I knew. I then proceeded to explain about Reiki and offered to give her the initiations so we would both be able to breathe a bit better when the weather was not so brilliant. I was also counting on the calming effect of Reiki on Jean during my driving which would benefit both of us.

The effect of Reiki on Jean's asthmatic condition was truly amazing. After the first day of the Reiki workshop she did not need to use the inhaler she normally used twice a day. For a while Jean stopped using her inhaler completely, but her doctor was worried and talked her into using it once a day.

As Reiki had such a dramatic effect on Jean's health, she continued and learned second degree Reiki and opened a little practice in our acupuncturist's home. She even ended up treating Lynn with Reiki when she was feeling unwell. Jean is now having a treatment room built in her home.

Flying with Reiki

Returning by plane from Paris to London after a Reiki workshop, I sat down in my place. After a while I had the by now familiar sensation of a tightness around my chest and difficulty in breathing. I turned to the man in the seat next to me and asked him if he was suffering from asthma. He looked quite shocked and said, 'Are you a witch?', to which I answered: 'Certainly not!' I ended up treating him with distant Reiki all the way to Heathrow Airport. He was quite intrigued and carried my luggage all the way to the Underground.

To develop this kind of sensitivity is quite normal if you practise some kind of energy work for a long time, not just Reiki. It is an extension of what you feel in yourself or when you have your hands on somebody during a Reiki treatment. Normally I do not notice something if it is not a serious condition or a strong emotional state. You can also tune into the state of somebody at a distance or in a picture if you choose to do so.

An Accident in a Greyhound Bus

I was travelling across the US in a Greyhound bus once when a woman slipped on the floor when coming out of the toilet in the back of the bus. She fell so badly that she injured her back and could not move. The bus driver stopped the bus and called for an ambulance to transport the injured woman to a hospital.

I had just recently learned Reiki and I was deliberating whether or not I should offer healing to the woman. Finally, I decided that I could offer it and let her decide. I was not thinking of curing her back but rather of treating her for the shock she suffered from the fall and lying immobile in the aisle of the bus.

I went up to the woman and asked if I could give her some healing. She looked quite frightened and I could see what was going on in her mind – that she could not cope with another strange thing happening to her. When she declined my offer, I asked if she wanted me to hold her hand instead. This time her answer was yes. As I held her hand, I could feel her heart energy settle and I stayed with her until she was taken away in the ambulance.

For me there was no difference in what was offered, but this incident taught me the importance of how you introduce Reiki. It is not necessary to explain about Reiki being a several-thousand-year-old Japanese Buddhist system learned through initiations in India from a Swedish person. It is enough to touch and let the Reiki flow.

A Motorbike Accident in Nairobi

I was invited for dinner at the home of some friends in Nairobi. The host, Oscar, wanted to post a letter before eating and went off on his motorbike. His sister and I waited but he didn't come back. I think an hour or so had passed when somebody phoned to tell us that there had been a traffic accident involving Oscar.

It took quite some time to locate the hospital to which Oscar had been taken. He was lying in a ward waiting for a surgeon to come – it was late at night by now. On Oscar's forehead there was a gaping wound. One of his legs was also injured but I was more worried about his head injury.

Oscar was still conscious and kept talking and moving non-stop as if not really aware of the seriousness of his injuries. As I started giving him Reiki on his heart area for shock, he felt very cold. Nobody stopped me giving him Reiki and I felt as though I was standing there for hours. He was taken away for x-rays and I could hear him screaming in pain in the distance; it was eerie. Even while his fore-head was being sewn together, I was allowed to do Reiki and talk and comfort him.

Only when the surgeon came to operate on the leg did his sister and I have to leave.

The healing process was long but Oscar did a lot of Reiki work himself on his leg. After a year he was fine. For me, it is not too important to know exactly what part Reiki played in the healing process. The value is more in the feeling that you can do something useful in situations like this. Often you get the feeling that you were meant to be there.

Reiki Attracts People
Who Want to be Healed

It seems Reiki draws me to certain people and places. I will go wher-ever I am invited to teach Reiki which has led me to meet and visit a lot of interesting people and places. Reiki is more than work, it is a lifestyle.

Sometimes the opposite seems to happen, people who need heal-ing get attracted to me. In France Midsummer's Night is celebrated with all kinds of live music and dancing in the streets, it is the 'Fête de la musique'. Saint John is celebrated on the next day by building bonfires – 'les feux de la Saint Jean'.

Once, when taking part in this celebration, I was sitting in the village of St Sylvain in front of a big bonfire listening to African drumming. People were walking around the fire throwing big home-made dolls into the fire. I believe this signified the cleansing of bad spirits of the winter months.

A little girl with Down's syndrome suddenly plonked herself on my lap, took my hand and put it on her stomach saying stomach-ache in French. I kept my hand on her stomach as she comfortably nestled in my lap as if we were old friends. After a while her father came looking for her. She did not want to leave me and it was only when they were going home that she reluctantly followed him.

Healing After an Abortion

While living in Totnes, I once came back from London on the train. As there were not enough taxis at the station, I decided to share a taxi with another woman. We did not talk much in the car since we were both tired from the journey. When we reached my place I said '... and if you need some healing here is my phone number and you know now where I live.' I could not believe what had come out of my mouth. Normally I would not pounce on a person like that.

The next day the woman phoned me. She had had an abortion the week before and was going through hell emotionally. For a week she came every day for a Reiki session. Her living situation was extremely complicated and she felt it was impossible to bring a child into that situation. Because, on the other hand, she really wanted the child, there were many emotional issues to be faced and many tears were shed.

After a week she went back to France where she lived. A few years later I ran into her by chance in Totnes and it was good to see her in a much happier state.

Reiki Gatherings

A common custom among people who practise Reiki is to meet up and exchange Reiki.

When I lived in Totnes, I used to have Reiki reunions or Reiki parties once a week. It was an open house from six o'clock to midnight for all my Reiki students. I put three to four mattresses on the floor for people to do Reiki. People were also asked to bring healthy snacks because sometimes you can get extremely hungry while giving or receiving Reiki. We put the food on a table in the kitchen and people could take breaks whenever they felt like it.

We would do group treatments in which one person is treated with Reiki by many people at the same time. It is a wonderful feeling, a bit like floating. Because group treatment is so much stronger, these sessions were much shorter. People took turns being patients. It was a social event too, with people chatting, giggling and feeling high or drunk from the energy.

When people were leaving I had to warn them to drive carefully. I remember that, even the next day, I used to feel extremely good.

ELEVEN

REIKI COMBINED with Other Methods of Healing

Reiki can be combined with any other healing method; nothing is contraindicated. Reiki just means life force – it is totally natural. Whatever healing or body work you do will only be enhanced by Reiki.

Once you are initiated, you cannot actually turn off the Reiki. It is part of your energy system. I will give examples of how Reiki can add an extra dimension to other alternative healing and educational systems of which I have personal experience. Reiki can also be very successfully combined with orthodox medicine.

Reiki and Massage

Having learned Reiki, I became curious about other alternative treatments. I started a three month course of Swedish massage. During the course I taught Reiki to many of my fellow students. While giving massage there was a marked difference in the heat of the hands of the students who had Reiki and those who did not. The clients would say, 'Oh, you have nice warm hands!'

Of course, massage from somebody who has Reiki has the added effect of the healing energy penetrating on a deeper level at the same time as the muscle tension is released. When working on a Swedish health farm, I gave a very perceptive little old lady a massage. After the massage, she asked me, 'What was that other thing coming out of your fingers?'

The only difference is that a pure Reiki session is somewhat stronger than a massage with Reiki coming through, since the hands are in contact with the body the whole time.

In addition to the healing aspect, another great thing about having the Reiki initiation for people doing other kinds of body work is the protection from taking on negative energy. Because the Reiki is flowing while you have body contact, you will get less tired as well.

Reiki, Alexander Techniques and Bad Backs

Alexander Technique is a system of re-education in which we are taught to become conscious of our habits and how we use ourselves in daily activities. Along with verbal instructions, the Alexander teacher uses his hands to guide the pupil in her movements to bring about better coordination.

When treating people with bad back problems, I used Reiki to help ease tension and release backs that had gone into spasm. Even when bones had gone out of their proper alignment, they would return once the muscles were released. Normally, I would only need three Reiki sessions on consecutive days.

One time, I treated an elderly Australian woman whose whole back had seized up even more after somebody had tried to 'undo' her muscle spasm with massage. She could not move at all. When somebody has had the wrong treatment there is, understandably, a lot of fear involved. Because of the non-invasive and non-doing character of Reiki, it was perfect for this case. It took about a month of regular Reiki treatments to open up her back again and for her to regain mobility. She ended up learning Reiki herself, as do most people who have experienced amazing healings.

The problem with Reiki and back problems was that people with tension in their backs would come back to me again and again with the same condition. I remember a temperamental woman I treated for recurrent back problems. I always wondered what she did to tighten up her back again. When I saw her shouting at somebody, I knew. That is when I became interested in the Alexander work, in which you learn to become conscious of your habits and how you create problems for yourself.

Having the Reiki initiations would not change the way an Alexander teacher teaches. In my experience it would only affect the quality of the touch. As with massage, I once had an Alexander teacher ask me what the other energy was while I was working on him on a table. It is a very subtle difference.

I also feel that Reiki helps open up the intuition and sensitivity that is important in the Alexander work. It is just part of you if you have the Reiki initiations – a bonus.

Reiki and Qi Gong

Qi Gong, consisting of sets of special exercises and meditations, is the traditional Chinese way of strengthening health, curing illness, prolonging life, improving mental health and achieving high levels of self-realisation. Qi means energy or life force, and the word Gong means cultivate or accumulate.

For me Reiki and Qi Gong are closely related. Both are ancient oriental systems taught through initiation or transmission from a teacher and are based in similar traditions. Both are spiritual practices in which the main purpose is healing, in the fullest sense of the word.

The main difference is the moving aspect in the Qi Gong practice, which is a great complement to the Reiki practice in which you sit still for hours. Because people who are initiated into Reiki are used to sensing energy, it is very easy to teach them Qi Gong.

I also want to mention that while practising Qi Gong with my Qi Gong Masters Zhixing and Zhendi Wang, I have learned and deepened my understanding about subtle energy work and come to understand more about the workings of Reiki.

Acupuncture and Reiki

Acupuncture, like Qi Gong, has its roots in Chinese medicine. Instead of movements, the insertion of needles is used to manipulate or balance the energy flowing in channels or meridians.

People ask me why I want to learn all these different systems when I know Reiki. For me, it is my passion to learn more about how subtle energy works. I find that the systems and traditions I learn are related to and complement each other.

I find acupuncture quicker for acute and very specific complaints. It is also a great combination with Reiki. When I started having acupuncture, I never thought about the fact that you, as a patient, would get the acupuncturist's energy through the needles. Now, with more experience, I find that this is obvious. So not only can an acupuncturist with Reiki give hands-on healing while the needles are in the patient, but the energy going into the needles will be purer and stronger.

I once gave Reiki to two patients who were HIV positive. At the same time, they were treated with acupuncture by another practitioner to strengthen their immune systems. When I put my hands on their feet, I had the most curious feeling. It was like plugging my hands into an energy field that was already in existence. What I also felt was the emotional turmoil these men were going through, both having been sacked from their jobs because of their condition. I could feel the soothing effect of the Reiki taking place. It felt like two channels going on at the same time.

Bach Remedies, Homeopathy and Herbs

Bach Flower Remedies consist of 38 different natural herbal remedies diluted as in homeopathic preparations so that they have a vibrational effect on 38 different kinds of negative emotional states.

When I first started treating a number of people with emotional problems, I used to prescribe Bach Remedy drops to be taken between treatments for quicker results. It is easy to prescribe the appropriate remedies since you get to know a person's particular problem very well while treating them.

I know a Reiki practitioner who sends many of her patients to get homeopathic remedies from another practitioner and finds that Reiki and homeopathy make an excellent combination. The only problem when doing combined treatment is knowing which treatment did what, if that is important.

A bottle of any homeopathic or Bach remedy, or herbs themselves, can be held in the hands of a Reiki practitioner for the Reiki to be soaked up and enhance the remedy. Some people use this technique even for orthodox drugs to minimise bad side effects. Crystals can also be empowered by Reiki, both by holding them in your hands and using mental programming on them.

Reiki and Orthodox Medicine

It is important, when practising complementary medicine, not to keep people from following orthodox medicine or telling them to stop conventional drug treatment. This matter is between them and their doctors. Reiki sometimes has miraculous results, but healing is not something that you as a practitioner can promise your patient – it is not in your hands.

If a person wants to use only complementary methods in their healing, that is his or her personal choice. This usually involves working on many levels apart from Reiki, such as lifestyle changes including exercise, diet, looking at the spiritual dimension of life and starting to practise systems such as yoga or Qi Gong. Also, a combination of complementary therapies might be necessary.

There is no contraindication to using Reiki alongside conventional medicine. The following case is an example of this.

Reiki and Radiotherapy

Jan, a woman in her early fifties, was diagnosed as having cervical cancer at the end of January 1996. As surgery was not an option, a series of 30 sessions of radiotherapy was planned. Treatment started at the end of February and took place every day except for weekends.

Friends of Jan's in Germany told her about a healing system called Reiki and advised Jan to find a Reiki practitioner in England as soon as possible. Jan found it difficult to come across any information about Reiki. A chance conversation with a colleague revealed that she had heard about Reiki and suggested phoning The South London Natural Healing Centre.

In the middle of March, Jan started receiving Reiki treatments. By this time she had received 18 sessions of radiotherapy and was feeling very unwell. Her Reiki practitioner, Migi, recommended that she see a homeopath at the same time as having Reiki. Jan had four Reiki sessions and felt that they helped to raise her energy level so that she was able to face the daily routine of visiting the hospital. Jan also suffered burns from the radiotherapy and these were eased considerably with Reiki. At first the burns were external but, later, internal too.

Jan entered the hospital in April to start internal radiotherapy. Migi made a Reiki home visit because Jan was so unwell. Because of Jan's poor condition, Migi suggested to Jan that she should take the Reiki initiations so she could treat herself every day. A few weeks later Jan was initiated by me into first degree Reiki.

Even though Jan gave herself Reiki every day, she continued her Reiki sessions with Migi once a month. Slowly during the summer, Jan started to regain her strength and the burns started to heal with the help of Reiki. In September 1996, Jan started attending Qi Gong classes at The South London Natural Health Centre.

Jan believes her recovery from the damaging effects of radiotherapy was accelerated through Reiki treatments. She thinks that Reiki minimized some of the possible damage to her bowel and her bladder. Jan is also in no doubt that Reiki helped to heal both the tumour and the effects of the radiotherapy. The latest scan shows no sign of the tumour. Another benefit of the Reiki is that Jan is no longer experiencing headaches, which had been a long-term problem.

Now Jan looks great!

TWELVE

HOW TO FIND A
Reiki Master

When Takata passed away in December 1980, she left her grand-daughter, Phyllis Lei Furumoto, as her successor.

Phyllis had received the first degree Reiki initiations as a child and she used to give her grandmother Reiki treatments when she visited. In the spring of 1979, Takata initiated Phyllis as a Master. Phyllis travelled and learned from Takata during the last two years of Takata's life in preparation for her own future role.

In the spring of 1982, a group of Takata's original 22 masters gathered in Hawaii to honour their teacher and the gift they had received from her. The meeting took place on the big island; Takata's ashes are kept here in the Buddhist Temple where she used to worship. The feeling of unity they gained from coming together led to annual meetings.

During their next gathering in 1983, The Reiki Alliance was created in order to honour and protect The Usui System of Reiki Healing, and to acknowledge Phyllis Lei Furumoto as the Grand Master in the direct spiritual lineage of Mikao Usui, Chujiro Hayashi, and Hawayo Takata.

There has been an explosion of Reiki around the world. The main difference between Reiki now and when Takata was alive is that during that time only the Reiki Grand Master could initiate others as Reiki Masters. Now, senior Reiki Masters, who have practised for many years and are ready to teach this degree, can initiate others to what is sometimes called the third degree – being a Reiki Master who can give the initiations.

Although first and second degree Reiki are taught in Reiki workshops, becoming a Reiki Master is a more long-term project. It usually takes the form of an informal apprenticeship with a chosen teacher. The master candidate needs to practise Reiki for several years to gain sufficient experience to guide and teach other people.

A process of self-purification also happens through Reiki practice. A Reiki Master needs to have worked through, or at least be quite aware of, personal issues. If a Reiki Master is not properly prepared and aligned with the Reiki lineage, the initiations that he gives will not be as powerful as they should be.

The Reiki Alliance gives guidelines for the delicate process of becoming a Reiki Master and acts as a support group for people who are already Reiki Masters. They will also only accept members who follow these and other professional standards, such as a code of ethics and a statement of identity.

A list of hundreds of Reiki Masters all around the world is published yearly by the Reiki Alliance. At present the Alliance has two offices, one in the US and one in Europe:

THE REIKI ALLIANCE

PO Box 41
Cataldo, Idaho 83810–1041
USA
Telephone: 1 208–682–3535
Fax: 1 208–682–4848

Honthorststraat # 40 11
1071 AM Amsterdam
Netherlands
Telephone: + 31(0) 294 290022
Fax: + 31(0) 294 290931

The Power of the Word
of Mouth

The traditional way of finding your Reiki Master has always been through word of mouth. Takata was against advertising; she felt the Reiki itself should attract people. I have always liked this concept in Reiki. Somebody has a powerful experience with Reiki and tells somebody else who learns Reiki and tells somebody else. This means not having to talk somebody into doing something, but the work itself drawing people to it.

I have seen many examples of this. Often whole families come to be initiated one by one. The most extreme example of the power of the word of mouth that I have come across is the case of a recovered alcoholic who spends most of his days in a café in Northern Paris. After he was initiated into Reiki, he talked about it to the people working in the café and to the customers. In a short time I had initiated the waiter, the waiter's sister, mother and girlfriend, the café owner, the café owner's wife and the café owner's brother-in-law who wanted to do Reiki on his three hundred sheep. I also started to initiate other people who had drinking problems and spent time in the café. Even the owner of a nearby café came for the initiation.

The interesting thing about this experience was that these people were not interested in complementary therapies or in living an alternative lifestyle.

I have shown you two ways of finding a Master – firstly the formal way, and secondly through trusting life itself to find your teacher. As far as finding a Reiki practitioner who can give treatments but not initiations, Reiki is now offered in nearly every complementary health centre.

Why not try it!

THIRTEEN

THE SPIRITUAL
Principles
of·Reiki

As you remember from Dr Usui's life story and his experience in the slum area, the beggars he treated did not feel any appreciation for their healing, nor did they want to change their lives. Out of this experience came Dr Usui's five spiritual principles of Reiki. These are guidelines on how to live our lives and are closely connected to our health in the broadest sense.

They might seem simple, but they are not always so easy to follow. Use them to meditate on.

Just for Today Do Not Anger

This does not mean that we should repress our anger. It means that we should be more conscious of our feelings and try to communicate them in a constructive way – not dump and displace our anger on others who have nothing to do with it.

When we start our healing process a lot of pent-up anger can be released. Whenever there is a mismatch between the intensity of the feelings and the event that has taken place, we know that there are a lot of unconscious feelings bubbling up to the surface.

The more we connect ourselves to the real love inside, the faster we can let go of anger and other negative emotions. There is nothing wrong with feeling emotions. Emotions are just energy that keeps moving. It is when they get stuck that we can become ill.

Just for Today Do Not Worry

Worrying never helps any issue or situation. It only creates tension and stress in the body. If we truly realize this, we can drop the worrying like a bad habit.

Just for today, we can try to experience the support that is all around us. If we worry a lot, it shows us our disconnectedness from the divine; there is a lack of trust. Use whatever means you know to connect again: prayer, meditation, Reiki.

Honour Your Teachers, Parents and Elders

We learn from our parents and teachers. When we take their knowledge inside us, it becomes part of us. So to honour our parents and teachers is to honour ourselves.

My parents always supported me, even if sometimes they did not understand what I was doing. I will always be grateful for that. Even if some people do not agree with everything their parents did, they in their turn were victims of their parents. So we have to look upon them with understanding and compassion. To keep blaming them is to be locked into a reactive pattern.

Thinking of my teachers, I feel enormous gratitude. There is no way to pay them back for their precious gifts. I can only try to follow their teachings.

Earn Your Living Honestly

We must live our lives in a way that keeps us true to ourselves. We will reap the fruits of our actions ourselves, nobody else will. The moral way in which we conduct our lives will, in its widest sense, reflect on our health.

Honesty is not just keeping to the facts. It is honouring our deepest feelings and beliefs and being aligned to the God-power inside.

Show Gratitude to All Living Things

In Reiki we always end a treatment by saying, 'Thank you, thank you, thank you!' This is to acknowledge the work of the spiritual energy. We, as channels, did not do anything and there is neither praise nor blame.

We are all inter-connected through this energy – people, animals and plants. When we truly realize this, we will live with more compassion and love, our real state of being.

AFTER WORDS

How This Book Came To Be

A few years back I had a dream. I dreamt about Takata trying to sort out her papers. In the dream she turned to me and said, 'I want you to become my secretary and organize my papers.' My immediate response to this request was, while still dreaming, 'I cannot possibly do this, I am dyslexic and I cannot even spell.'

Then, a little over a year ago, my astrologer, Sue, asked me if I was interested in writing a book about Reiki. She had heard that an agent was looking for somebody who had practised Reiki for a long time. I heard myself say, 'I am dyslexic and cannot even spell, so I do not think I can do it. And anyway Reiki is an oral tradition so what is there to write?'

I listened to what I was saying and it seemed to have a familiar ring, then I remembered my dream. I thought to myself that if this book wanted to be written, I myself should not stop it. I should let the universe stop me. If I was meant to write the book, Reiki itself would support it. I asked for the phone number of the agent. Sue gave me a contact number and very soon I had the agent, Susan, on the line. Yes, she was interested in me writing about Reiki, so first of all I had to write a synopsis.

It all felt nebulous to me since I had never done this kind of thing before. Since Susan had a horse with an infected foot, I suggested that we meet and I could initiate her into Reiki. She would be able to work on the horse with Reiki and understand what this healing was about. We would also be able to talk and I would understand more about how I should proceed.

Susan lives in the country in a beautiful converted little church. I did the initiations in the tower room. During the Reiki treatment I gave Sue, it started to snow and when we opened our eyes the whole countryside was covered in white. It was magical!

When I came back to London, I contacted my Reiki Master, Wanja, to ask what her feelings were on writing about Reiki. She supported the project and said it was OK to write it from my perspective and share my experiences. Then I faxed my Spiritual Teacher to ask for her blessings. Honour your teachers …

Writing the synopsis was easy, it sort of happened by itself. Getting a ride home in a car from my meditation centre, I talked about my project and that I needed some help with the editing. A woman, Diana, whom I knew slightly, was also in the car and turned out to be an editor. She said she would be happy to help me. I initiated her and her husband into first and second degree in exchange.

Then it was a long time until the synopsis was accepted by a publisher. I almost forgot about it for a while. I felt I could not do anything until I had a contract and could buy a computer with a spell check button. In the end, I had only three months to complete the manuscript. I bought a computer without any knowledge of how to use it and I could not even type.

During the 14 days that it took for me to learn to use the computer, my laptop was my constant companion. My family and friends were very helpful. Anybody with computer skills was teaching me what he or she knew. I did not attend dinner parties unless I could bring my computer. While travelling on a train, I was afraid that a passenger would spill coffee on my precious machine, and told him so – I was an obsessed woman. He happened to be a computer expert, and proceeded to teach me anything I wanted to know for three hours between Gothenburg and Malmö.

When my files were in order, one file for each chapter, I started to write. I always started by doing mental Reiki for the creative energy to flow. While doing this one time, I received the message: 'In the writing we will come through.' My experience of writing has been like giving Reiki to the computer. Instead of squeezing 30,000 words out of my brain, I have had the feeling of them falling out of my heart. While writing, I have had to contact many of my old Reiki students and friends to make their stories as accurate as possible. It has been an incredible healing experience.

I hope I have been able to convey Reiki as an exciting experience to you.

Thank you for being with me in this adventure! Never forget the magic in life.

As the old warrior said in Star Wars: 'May the force be with you!'

USEFUL ADDRESSES
and Websites

The Reiki Association

2 Manor Cottages
Stockley Hill
Peterchurch
Hereford HR2 0SF
Telephone and Fax: 01584 891 197
Alternative telephone: 01981 550 829
e-mail: reikiassoc_admin@compuserve.com
www.reikiassociation.org.uk

The Reiki Alliance

US Office:
The Reiki Alliance
PO Box 41
Cataldo
Idaho 83810–1041
Telephone: 1 208 783 3535
Fax: 1 208 783 4848
e-mail: ReikiAlliance@compuserve.com
www.reikialliance.org.uk

European Office:
Stichting The Reiki Alliance – Europe Office
PO Box 75523
1070 AM Amsterdam
Netherlands
Telephone: + 31 (0) 294 290022
Fax + 31 (0) 294 290931
e-mail: 100125.466@compuserve.com

Reiki Outreach International
PO Box 191156
San Diego
CA 92159–1156
USA
Telephone: + 1 916 863 1500
www.annieo.com/reikioutreach

Further Reading

Fran Brown. *Living Reiki, Takata's Teachings*, LifeRhythm, Mendocino, California, USA, 1992

Helen J. Haberly. *Reiki: Hawayo Takata's Story*, Archedigm, Olney, Maryland, USA, 1990

Wanja Twan. *In the Light of a Distant Star*, Morning Star Productions, Vancouver, British Columbia, Canada, 1995

Guildford College
Learning Resource Centre

Please return on or before the last date shown
This item may be renewed by telephone unless overdue